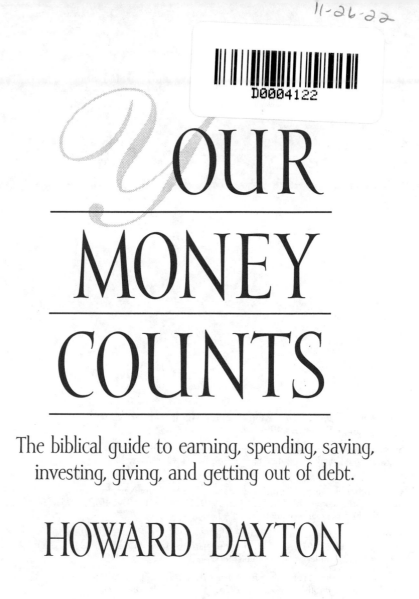

YOUR
MONEY
COUNTS

The biblical guide to earning, spending, saving,
investing, giving, and getting out of debt.

HOWARD DAYTON

Tyndale House Publishers, Inc.
Wheaton, Illinois

Library of Congress Catalog Card Number 95-83819
ISBN 0-8423-8592-4

Printed in the United States of America

07 06 05 04
11 10 9 8 7 6

To Bev, my wife,
God's choice gift to our family

To Matthew, my beloved son,
and to Danielle, a joy

To Jim Seneff, without his vision
this book would never have been conceived

To Will Norton, without his skill
this book would never have been born

To Tim Manor, who is closer than a brother,
and George Fooshee, my mentor

To the Crown Ministries Family, precious co-laborers,
you mean more to me than I can ever say

CONTENTS

THE PROBLEM

ALLEN AND JEAN HITCHCOCK decided to end their marriage of 24 years.

In anticipation of the divorce settlement, Allen began to review the family's financial records. As he sorted through the files, he came across an old faded check made out to the hotel where he and Jean had stayed on their honeymoon. Another check had paid for an installment on their first car. He picked up still another check and remembered with fatherly pride how he had written it out to the hospital when their daughter was born. And then there was the down payment on their first home. . . .

After several hours of sorting through such checks, Allen realized how much he and his wife had invested in their marriage. He paused, deep in thought for several minutes. Then he closed the file and dialed his wife's number. After an awkward exchange he blurted out the reason for his call. Would she work with him to rebuild their marriage?

While a family crisis such as Allen and Jean's may be foreign to some of us, the message of their family's checks is common. It is the story of our lives. It tells of our values, how much we save, what we spend, to whom we give. In fact, our checkbooks tell us more about our priorities than does anything else.

That's why Jesus talked so much about money. Sixteen of the 38 parables were concerned with how to handle money and possessions. Indeed, Jesus Christ said more about money than about almost any other subject. The Bible offers 500 verses on prayer, fewer than 500 verses on faith, but more than 2,350 verses on money and possessions.

The Lord said a lot about it because He wants us to know His perspective on this critical area of life. He dealt with money matters because *money does matter*.

TWO

THE ANSWER–
THE BIBLE IS A BLUEPRINT FOR LIVING

I WAS SLIDING PAPERS and reports into my briefcase when the phone rang on my desk. It was 5:30 p.m., and I was getting ready to go home after a long day of paperwork and personal conferences. I was tired. Reluctantly, I picked up the phone.

"Hello, Howard. This is Allen Hitchcock."

I felt a pang of embarrassment. I had neglected to return his earlier call. He sounded depressed, and I made a lame apology for not calling him back.

"Jean and I considered a divorce, but we decided to try to work it out," he said, his voice sounding strained.

Their financial problems were on the verge of destroying their marriage. He asked if we could meet to discuss their situation. We had become acquainted at church two years before, when they had moved from St. Louis to Orlando. Allen earned a middle-income salary as an assistant manager for a department store, but he couldn't understand where the money went. They faced increasing expenses for their growing family, and in a few years they would need college tuition for the children. Neither he nor Jean could foresee a brighter future.

In addition, the Hitchcocks owed a substantial amount to retail stores, doctors, credit card companies and their bank. They had a sizable home mortgage.

Because of their debts and their increasing daily expenses, the Hitchcocks shopped carefully, sometimes comparing half a dozen outlets for the best price. They used cents-off coupons at the supermarket. Allen did most of the automobile repairs, and Jean avoided buying expensive convenience foods. But the family faced a critical problem. Jean and Allen did not have a clear guideline for handling money. They never had been able to budget their spending. They seldom decided not to buy what they wanted, and they had no plan to save or invest for the future.

I understood their predicament. Several years before, a friend, Jim Seneff, and I found ourselves making daily financial decisions for our expanding businesses and young families without a scriptural point of reference. To be the best husbands and the best businessmen we could be, we felt compelled to do a thorough study of what Scripture said about money. Together we read the entire Bible, locating each of the 2,350 verses that dealt with money and arranging those verses by topics. Then we put this information into a seminar and presented it at our church. The response was remarkable. People bombarded us with questions and described several areas of intense frustration. Other churches asked for the seminar, and through the years the seminar developed into the Crown Ministries Small Group Financial Study, which is today conducted in churches throughout the nation.

It is through these small group studies that thousands of people like the Hitchcocks have been helped. We have found that most people—indeed, most Christians—either don't know or have not applied God's financial principles to their lives. Nevertheless, applying these principles is crucial for three reasons:

1. How we handle money affects our fellowship with the Lord.
In Luke 16:11 we read, "If therefore you have not been faithful in the use of worldly wealth, who will entrust the true riches to you?" In this verse Jesus equates how we handle our money with the quality of our spiritual life. If we handle our money properly according to the principles of Scripture, our fellowship with Christ will grow

stronger. However, if we manage money unfaithfully, our fellowship with Him will suffer.

Someone once told me that the Lord often allows a person to teach a subject because he or she desperately needs it. That is certainly true for me in the area of money. I have had the privilege of leading dozens of Crown small group studies, and I have never met anyone who had more wrong attitudes about money or who handled their finances more contrarily to Scripture than I did. When I learned these principles and applied them, I experienced a dramatic improvement in my fellowship with the Lord. Following God's financial principles draws us closer to Christ.

2. Possessions compete with the Lord.

Possessions are a primary competitor with Christ for lordship of our lives. Jesus tells us we must choose to serve only one of these two masters: "No one can serve two masters. Either he will hate the one and love the other, or he will be devoted to the one and despise the other. You cannot serve both God and money" (Matthew 6:24, NIV). It is impossible for us to serve money—even in a small way—and still serve the Lord.

When the Crusades were being fought during the 12th century, the crusaders employed mercenaries to fight on their behalf. Because it was a religious war, the crusaders insisted that the mercenaries be baptized before fighting. As they were being baptized, the mercenaries would hold their swords out of the water to symbolize the one thing in their life that Jesus Christ did not control. They had the freedom to use the swords in any way they wished.

Today many people handle their money in a similar fashion, though they may not be as obvious about it. They hold their wallet or purse "out of the water," in effect saying, *"God, You can be the Lord of my entire life except for my money. I am perfectly capable of handling that myself."*

3. Much of life revolves around the use of money.

During your normal week, how much time do you spend earning money in your job, making decisions on how to spend money, thinking about where to save and invest money or praying about your giving? Fortunately, God has prepared us adequately for these tasks by giving us the Bible as His blueprint for handling money.

THE ANSWER

Increasingly, people wonder where they can turn for help. There are two basic alternatives: the Bible and the answers people devise. The way most people handle money is in sharp contrast to God's financial principles. Isaiah 55:8 reads, "'For My thoughts are not your thoughts, neither are your ways My ways,' declares the Lord."

To help the reader recognize the differences between these two ways, a brief comparison appears at the end of each chapter under the heading "Contrast."

LEARNING TO BE CONTENT

Contentment is mentioned seven times in the Bible, and six of those refer to money. In Philippians 4:11-13 Paul writes,

> I have learned to be content whatever the circumstances. I know what it is to be in need, and I know what it is to have plenty. I have learned the secret of being content in any and every situation, whether well fed or hungry, whether living in plenty or in want. I can do everything through him who gives me strength (NIV).

Examine these verses carefully. We are not born with the instinct for contentment; rather, it is learned.

The purpose of this book is to help you learn the biblical principles of handling money and possessions. The book will offer you practical ways to integrate these principles into your life. As you discover these principles and put them into practice, you will draw closer to Christ, submit more fully to Him as Lord, learn to be content and set your financial house in order.

CONTRAST

Society says: God plays no role in handling money, and my happiness is based on being able to afford my desired standard of living.

Scripture says: As you learn and follow the scriptural principles of how to handle money, you will draw close to Christ and learn to be content in every circumstance.

GOD'S PART—
THE FOUNDATION

ON A RAINY NOVEMBER MORNING Allen and Jean Hitchcock arrived at my office to work through their financial problems in an attempt to save their marriage.

Allen and Jean were Christians, but they had never been exposed to the Bible's perspective on money and possessions. They appreciated their beautiful two-story brick house in suburban Orlando, their two late-model automobiles and their other possessions. Both felt that they had worked hard for what they had and that they had earned the right to enjoy "the good life." However, after financial pressures threatened their standard of living, their lack of contentment surfaced in a major marital crisis. A serious lack of communications existed about their family finances. Allen and Jean each had their own opinions on how to spend the family income, and they had never been able to discuss the subject without ending up in an argument.

They were close to losing everything to their creditors. That, coupled with the possibility of divorce, had jarred them from their complacency. So when I sat down with Allen and Jean on the Friday after Thanksgiving, they were motivated to learn what the Bible says about money.

Scripture teaches there are two distinct parts to the handling of our money: the part God plays and the part we play. I believe most of the confusion relating to the handling of money arises from the fact that these two parts are not clearly understood.

God's part is the foundation of contentment. In Scripture God calls Himself by more than 250 names. The name that best describes God's part in the area of money is *Master.* This is the most important chapter of the entire book because how we view God determines how we live. For example, after losing his children and all his possessions, Job was still able to worship God. He knew the Lord and the Lord's role as Master of those possessions. Similarly, Moses forsook the treasures of Egypt and chose to suffer mistreatment with the people of God. Both Job and Moses knew the Lord and accepted His role as Master.

Let's examine what the Bible has to say about God's part in three crucial areas: ownership, control and provision.

> *Everything in the heavens and earth is yours, O Lord, and this is your kingdom. We adore you as being in control of everything. Riches and honor come from you alone, and you are the Ruler of all mankind; your hand controls power and might, and it is at your discretion that men are made great and given strength.*
>
> KING DAVID,
> 1 CHRONICLES
> 29:11-12 (LB)

OWNERSHIP

The Bible clearly states that God is sole owner of everything. "The earth is the Lord's, and all it contains" (Psalm 24:1). Scripture even reveals specific items God owns. Leviticus 25:23 identifies Him as owner of all the land: "The land . . . shall not be sold permanently, for the land is Mine." Haggai 2:8 reveals that "'the silver is Mine, and the gold is Mine,' declares the Lord of hosts." And in Psalm 50:10, the Lord tells us: "For every beast of the forest is Mine, the cattle on a thousand hills."

The Lord is the Creator of all things, and He has never transferred the ownership of His creation to people. In Colossians 1:17 we are told that "in Him all things hold together." At this very moment the Lord literally holds everything together by His power.

Recognizing God's ownership is critical in allowing Jesus Christ to become the Lord of our money and possessions.

Ownership or Lordship?

If we are going to be genuine followers of Christ, we must transfer the ownership of our possessions to the Lord. "No one . . . can be My disciple who does not give up all his own possessions" (Luke 14:33). In my experience I have found that the Lord will sometimes test us by asking that we be willing to relinquish the very possession that is dearest to us.

Scripture's most vivid example of this is when the Lord told Abraham: "Take now your son, your only son, whom you love, Isaac . . . and offer him there as a burnt offering" (Genesis 22:2). When Abraham obeyed, demonstrating his willingness to give up his dearest possession, God provided a substitute ram for the offering, and Isaac was not harmed.

Outstanding author Larry Burkett observed, "When we acknowledge God's ownership, every spending decision becomes a spiritual decision. No longer do we ask, 'Lord, what do You want me to do with *my* money?' The question is restated, 'Lord, what do You want me to do with Your money?'" When we have this perspective, spending and saving decisions are equally as spiritual as giving decisions.

The First Step Toward Contentment

To learn to be content, you must recognize God as the owner of all your possessions. If you believe you own even a single possession, then the circumstances affecting that possession will be reflected in your attitude. If something favorable happens to that possession, then you will be happy. But if something bad occurs, you will be discontented.

After Jim Seneff went through the exercise of transferring ownership of everything he possessed to God, he bought a new car. It was just two days old when a young person drove into the side of it. Jim's first reaction was, "Well, God, I don't know why You want a dent in the side of Your new car, but You certainly have a big one!" Similarly, when John Wesley learned that his home had been destroyed by fire, he exclaimed, "The Lord's house burned. One less responsibility for me!"

Yet it is not easy to maintain this perspective consistently. It is far too easy to think that the possessions we have and the money we earn are entirely the result of our skills and achievements. We find it difficult not to believe we have earned the right to their ownership. *I am the master of my fate*, the humanist says. *I alone own my possessions.* Obviously, this view of ownership is the prevailing one in our culture.

Giving up ownership is not easy, nor is it a once-and-for-all transaction. We constantly need to be reminded that God owns all our possessions.

CONTROL

The second responsibility God has retained is ultimate control of every event that occurs upon the earth. Examine several of the names of God in Scripture: Master, Almighty, Creator, Shepherd, Lord of lords and King of kings. It's obvious who is in charge:

> We adore you as being in control of everything. Riches and honor come from you alone, and you are the Ruler of all mankind; your hand controls power and might, and it is at your discretion that men are made great and given strength (1 Chronicles 29:11-12, LB).

Psalm 135:6 reads, "Whatever the Lord pleases He does, in heaven and in earth." And in Daniel 4:34-35 King Nebuchadnezzar stated: "I praised the Most High . . . He does as he pleases with the powers of heaven and the peoples of the earth. No one can hold back his hand or say to him: 'What have you done?'" (NIV).

The Lord is in control of even difficult circumstances. "I am the Lord, and there is no other, the One forming light and creating darkness, causing well-being and creating calamity; I am the Lord who does all these" (Isaiah 45:6-7). It is important for the child of God to realize that his heavenly Father orchestrates even seemingly devastating circumstances for ultimate good in the lives of the godly. "And we know that God causes all things to work together for good to those who love God, to those who are called according to His purpose" (Romans 8:28).

The most traumatic times Bev and I have had in our marriage were when we were in the process of adopting our second son, Andrew. We received Andrew when he was four days old. He was an extraordinarily beautiful baby. When he was about three months old, we noticed that he appeared to have physical problems. We went through two months of a roller-coaster experience with physicians unable to agree on a diagnosis.

Finally, we learned that his natural mother had used powerful narcotics before and during the pregnancy, and Andrew had been born with only the stem of his brain. In our pain and deep hurt we repeatedly returned to the foundational fact that our heavenly Father loved Andrew even more than we did and that God wanted to entrust him into our care for a season. We became close friends with Andrew's natural grandparents, and our family learned compassion for the disadvantaged. We saw the Lord provide Andrew with the very best care, and we experienced many blessings in the midst of this emotional time. The Lord allows difficult circumstances for three reasons:

1. To accomplish His intentions. This is illustrated in the life of Joseph who, as a teenager, was sold into slavery by his jealous brothers. Years later Joseph told his brothers: "Do not be grieved or angry with yourselves, because you sold me here; for God sent me before you to preserve life . . . *it was not you who sent me here, but God*" (Genesis 45:5, 8, emphasis added).

2. To develop our character. Godly character, something that is precious in the sight of the Lord, is often developed in the midst of trying times. Romans 5:3-4 reads, "We also exult in our tribulations, knowing that tribulation brings about perseverance; and perseverance, proven character." Writing on this theme, A.W. Tozer said, "God can't use a person to the maximum, until he or she has been hurt deeply." I believe this is true. I've learned lessons of trusting the Lord and drawing close to Him that I never would have learned apart from difficult times.

3. To discipline His children. When we are disobedient, we can expect our loving Lord to administer discipline to encourage us to abandon our sin. This often comes through difficult circumstances.

For those whom the Lord loves He disciplines . . . He disciplines us for our good, that we may share His holiness. All discipline for the moment seems not to be joyful, but sorrowful; yet to those who have been trained by it, afterwards it yields the peaceful fruit of righteousness (Hebrews 12:6, 10-11).

The Lord has absolute control over every circumstance you will ever face. You can be content in knowing that your loving heavenly Father intends to use each situation ultimately for a good purpose.

PROVISION

The third element of God's part is that He has promised to provide our needs. "But seek ye first the kingdom of God, and his righteousness; and all these things [food and clothing] shall be added unto you" (Matthew 6:33, KJV). In Genesis 22:14, God is spoken of as "Jehovah-jireh," which means "the Lord will provide." He takes care of His people, and He does not need a prosperous economy to provide for them. Each day He gave manna to the children of Israel during their 40 years of wandering in the wilderness. Jesus fed 5,000 with only five loaves and two fish.

God is both predictable and unpredictable. He is absolutely predictable in His faithfulness to provide for our needs. What we cannot predict is how the Lord will provide. He uses various and sometimes surprising means of meeting our needs. He may increase our income, provide a gift or stretch our limited resources through money-saving purchases. Regardless of how He chooses to provide for our needs, He is utterly reliable.

First Timothy 6:8 tells us that our needs are food and covering. In other words, there is a difference between needs and wants. A need is a basic necessity of life—food, clothing or shelter. A want is anything more than a need. A steak dinner, a new car and the latest fashions are all wants.

God's part in helping us reach contentment is that He has obligated Himself to provide our needs. However, He has not promised to provide our wants. He promises to provide our needs, and He tells us to be content when these needs are met. "And if we have food and covering, with these we shall be content" (1 Timothy 6:8).

Let me illustrate God's provision with a story.

As World War II was drawing to a close, the Allied armies gathered up many hungry orphans. They were placed in camps where they were well-fed. Despite excellent care, they slept poorly. They seemed nervous and afraid. Finally, a psychologist came up with a solution. Each child was given a piece of bread to hold after he was put to bed. If he was hungry, more food was provided, but when he was finished, this particular piece of bread was just to be held—not eaten.

The piece of bread produced wonderful results. The children went to bed, instinctively knowing they would have food to eat the next day. That guarantee gave the children a restful and contented sleep.[1]

Similarly, the Lord has given us His guarantee—our "piece of bread." As we cling to His promises of provision, we can relax and be content. "And my God shall supply all your needs according to His riches" (Philippians 4:19). So even if you are in the middle of an extreme financial problem, you can be content because the Lord has promised to feed, clothe and shelter you.

I am convinced that the Lord will provide—at just the right time—the resources necessary for us to fulfill the purpose and calling He has for each of us. This is illustrated in 2 Samuel 12:7-8 when He spoke to David through Nathan the prophet: "Thus says the Lord God of Israel, 'It is I who anointed you king over Israel and it is I who delivered you from the hand of Saul. I also gave you your master's house and your master's wives into your care, and I gave you the house of Israel and Judah; and if that had been too little, I would have added to you many more things like these.'"

From the life of David we see that God did not provide all the necessary resources for him to be king all at once. They came at the appropriate time, as David needed them. Occasionally, the Lord has withheld resources from Crown Ministries. I sometimes have been confused when this has occurred. Later I discovered that if we had received them too soon, we would not have spent them wisely.

GETTING TO KNOW GOD

The basic reason we fail to recognize God's part is that we do not understand who God is. We often have no genuine awe for the Lord "who stretched out the heavens and laid the foundations of the earth" (Isaiah 51:13). We tend to shrink God down and fit Him into a mold with human abilities and limitations. However, we can expand our vision to capture the true perspective of God by studying what the Bible tells us about Him. The following is but a sample:

Lord of the Universe
The Lord's power is incomprehensible to humans. For example, astronomers estimate more than 100 billion galaxies exist in the universe, each containing billions of stars. The distance from one end of a galaxy to the other is often measured in millions of light years. The enormity of the universe is mind boggling. Isaiah 40:26 reads, "Lift up your eyes on high and see who has created these stars, the One who leads forth their host by number, He calls them all by name; because of the greatness of His might and the strength of His power not one of them is missing."

Lord of the Nations
Examine the Lord's role and position relative to nations and people. Isaiah 40:21-24 tells us, "Do you not know? Have you not heard? . . . It is He who sits above the vault of the earth, and its inhabitants are like grasshoppers. . . . He it is who reduces rulers to nothing, who makes the judges of the earth meaningless. Scarcely have they been planted . . . but He merely blows on them, and they wither."

And from Isaiah 40:15, 17 we read, "Behold, the nations are like a drop from a bucket, and are regarded as a speck of dust on the scales . . . All the nations are as nothing before Him, they are regarded by Him as less than nothing and meaningless."

Lord of the Individual

God is not an aloof, disinterested "force." Rather, He is intimately involved with each of us as individuals. Psalm 139:3-4, 16 reveals, "You are familiar with all my ways. Before a word is on my tongue you know it completely, O Lord . . . All the days ordained for me were written in your book before one of them came to be" (NIV). The Lord is so involved in our lives that He reassures us, "The very hairs of your head are all numbered" (Matthew 10:30). Our heavenly Father is the One who knows us best and loves us the most.

God hung the stars in space, fashioned the earth's towering mountains and mighty oceans, and determined the destiny of nations. Jeremiah observed correctly, "Nothing is too difficult for Thee" (Jeremiah 32:17). Yet God knows when a sparrow falls to the ground. He is the Lord of the infinite and the infinitesimal.

In summary, let's review what God's part is. He is the owner, He is in control of every circumstance, and He has promised to meet our needs. In other words, God who created the world and holds it together is able to perform His responsibilities and keep His promises. However, God's part is only half of the equation. It is the most important part, but it is only half. In the next chapter we will begin to examine the other half, our part.

CONTRAST

Society says: What I possess I alone own, and I alone control my destiny.

Scripture says: What I possess, God owns. He is the sovereign, living God who controls all events.

At the end of most chapters, after the CONTRAST between society and Scripture, there will be a COMMITMENT section that will give you the opportunity to practice the biblical principle we have just covered. I challenge and encourage you to do the COMMITMENT sections because they will help make the principles a part of your life.

COMMITMENT

In the Crown Ministries small group study we go through an exercise of transferring the ownership of our possessions to the Lord. We use a deed to do this because a deed is often used to transfer the ownership of property.

When participants in the Crown study complete and sign the deed, they are acknowledging that God is owner of their assets. The exercise is important because we all occasionally forget that God owns everything. We act as if we own it all. By signing the deed, a person establishes a specific time when God's ownership is acknowledged. Thus, a person can refer to the document repeatedly and recall that God owns everything.

The following will help you complete the deed:

1. Insert today's date.
2. Print your name. You are the one transferring ownership.
3. The Lord is the One receiving the assets.
4. Give prayerful consideration to the possessions you wish to acknowledge God owns. Then list those items.
5. Sign your name.
6. On the lower right-hand corner there is a space for the signature of two witnesses. These friends can help hold you accountable for recognizing God as owner of your possessions.

QUIT-CLAIM DEED

THIS QUIT-CLAIM DEED,

MADE THE _____ DAY OF _____ , 19_____

FROM:

TO: THE LORD

I (WE) HEREBY TRANSFERE TO THE LORD THE OWNERSHIP OF THE FOLLOWING POSESSIONS:

WITNESSES WHO WILL HELP HOLD ME (US) ACCOUNTABLE IN THE RECOGNITION OF GOD'S OWNERSHIP:

_____

_____

_____

STEWARDS OF THE POSSESIONS ABOVE:

_____

_____

OUR PART—
GOOD AND FAITHFUL

AFTER HE AND JEAN FINISHED signing the deed, Allen slid it across the desk. "I feel a lot of relief," he said. "But I also feel like I'm supposed to do something." Allen was right. We cannot just sit back, do nothing and wait for God to perform. We have a responsibility. But, like Allen, we may not know exactly what our part is.

God, the Master, is the owner of everything, the controller of all events and our provider. Our responsibility is to be a steward. The word for *steward* can be translated into two different words: *manager* and *supervisor*. In Scripture the position of a steward is one of great responsibility. He or she is the supreme authority under the master and has full responsibility for all the master's possessions and household affairs.

> *Well done, good and faithful slave; you were faithful with a few things, I will put you in charge of many things, enter into the joy of your master.*
> MATTHEW 25:21

As we examine Scripture we see that God, as Master, has given us the authority to be stewards. "You [God] have put him [people] in charge of everything you made; everything is put under his authority" (Psalm 8:6, LB).

One's only responsibility is to be faithful. "Moreover it is required in stewards, that a man be found faithful" (1 Corinthians 4:2, KJV). Before we can be faithful, we must know what we are required to do. Just as the purchaser of an automobile studies the manufacturer's manual to learn how to properly operate the car, we need to examine the Creator's handbook, the Bible, to find out how He wants us to handle His possessions. Several elements of faithfulness are important to understand.

> Contentment is the by-product of the faithful discharge of our duties.

1. Faithful With All Our Resources

We are charged to be faithful in handling 100 percent, not just 10 percent. Unfortunately, many churches have concentrated only on teaching how to handle 10 percent of our income—the area of giving. Although this area is crucial, we have allowed Christians to learn how to handle the other 90 percent from the world's perspective, not from our Lord's perspective.

Because they do not know how to handle money biblically, many Christians have wrong attitudes about possessions and make incorrect financial decisions that lead to painful consequences. Hosea 4:6 reads, "My people are destroyed for lack of knowledge." Ignorance of or disobedience to scriptural financial principles frequently causes money problems.

2. Faithful Regardless of How Much We Have

The issue in Scripture is how to handle faithfully all God has entrusted to us. The faithful steward is responsible for what he or she has, whether it is much or little. The parable of the talents illustrates this. "For it is just like a man about to go on a journey, who called his own slaves, and entrusted his possessions to them. And to one he gave five talents, to another, two, and to another, one . . ." (Matthew 25:14-15). When the master returned, he held each slave accountable for managing his possessions faithfully. The master commended the faithful slave who received the five talents: "Well done, good and faithful slave; you were faithful with a few things, I will put you in charge of many things, enter into the joy of your master" (Matthew 25:21). Interestingly, the slave who had been given two talents received a reward equal to that given to the slave who had been given the five talents (see Matthew 25:23). We are required to be faithful whether we are given much or little. As someone once said, "It's not what I would do if one million dollars were my lot; it's what I am doing with the ten dollars I've got."

3. Faithfulness in Little Things
Luke 16:10 reads, "He who is faithful in a very little thing is faithful also in much; and he who is unrighteous in a very little thing is unrighteous also in much." How do you know if a child is going to take good care of his first car? Observe how he cared for his bicycle. How do you know if a salesperson will do a competent job of serving a large client? Observe how he or she served a small client. If we have the character to be faithful with small things, the Lord knows He can trust us with greater responsibilities.

"Small things are small things," Hudson Taylor, the missionary statesman, said, "but faithfulness with a small thing is a big thing."

4. Faithfulness With Another's Possessions
Faithfulness with another's possessions will, in some measure, determine the amount with which you are entrusted. "And if you have not been faithful in the use of that which is another's, who will give you that which is your own?" (Luke 16:12). This is a principle that is often overlooked. Are you faithful with another's possessions? Are you careless with your employer's office supplies? Do you waste electricity when you are staying in a motel room? When someone allows you to use something, are you careful to return it in good shape? I am certain some people have not been given more because they have been unfaithful with the possessions of others.

5. Faithfulness Builds Character
God uses money to refine our character. In 1918 David McConaughy wrote a book, *Money, the Acid Test.* In it he said:

> Money, most common of temporal things, involves uncommon and eternal consequences. Even though it may be done quite unconsciously, money molds people—in the process

of getting it, of saving it, of using it, of giving it, of accounting for it. Depending upon how it is handled, it proves a
blessing or a curse to its possessor; either the person
becomes master of the money, or the money becomes master of the person.

Our Lord takes money, the thing that, essential though
it is to our common life, sometimes seems so sordid, and he
makes it a touchstone to test the lives of people and an
instrument for molding them into the likeness of himself.[2]

Clearly, if we are handling our possessions as faithful stewards,
our character is being built. If we are unfaithful, our character is
being torn down. Richard Halverson said it precisely: "Jesus Christ
said more about money than any other single thing because money
is of first importance when it comes to a person's real nature. Money
is an exact index to our true character. Throughout Scripture we
find an intimate correlation between the development of a person's
character and how he or she handles money."[3]

6. Faithfulness Leads to Contentment

Once we know God's part and our part and faithfully do our part,
we can be content. In Philippians we discover that Paul has learned
to be content because he knew that God would supply all his needs
(Philippians 4:19), and he had been faithful. "The things you have
learned and received and heard and seen in me, practice these
things" (Philippians 4:9).

As we apply the principles of God's economy, we will begin to
get out of debt, spend more wisely, start saving for our future goals
and give even more to the work of Christ. The Bible offers real solu-
tions to today's financial problems. Each of the following chapters
deals with one of the specific areas necessary to equip us to become
faithful stewards.

At the beginning of most of the remaining chapters we will
complete a section of the "wheel of faithfulness" shown here to help
clarify the responsibilities of a faithful steward.

CONTRAST

Society says: You earned your money, now spend it any way you choose and you'll be happy.

Scripture says: You can only be content if you have been a faithful steward handling money from the Lord's perspective.

DEBT—
ACT YOUR OWN WAGE

T HE MOST IMMEDIATE financial problem facing Allen and Jean was pressure from their creditors. And creditors they had! They had two loans from a bank, bills from three department stores and an outstanding balance on an assortment of credit cards. And then there was the home mortgage.

The Hitchcocks' indebtedness started soon after they had married when they applied for their first loan. Jean, who grew up in a wealthy family, said, "Our friends had new cars, and we felt deprived. We had to have a new car too." Later, when they were transferred to Orlando, they bought a house in the suburbs, borrowing for the down payment. The debts continued to pile up. "Finally," Jean said, "the man from the bank told us he was going to take our house and garnish [take from] Allen's salary."

> Any government, like any family, can for a year spend a little more than it earns. But you and I know that a continuance of that habit means the poorhouse.
> FRANKLIN D.
> ROOSEVELT, 1932

"Most of our debts were accumulated so slowly through the years," Allen said, "that we didn't realize what was happening until it was too late."

Each year millions of people find themselves in the Hitchcocks' predicament. A credit expert says the major reason is "damage to the borrower's ability to pay." People take out loans on the assumption they will have a steady flow of income; then, the unexpected happens. Someone gets sick. A new baby is on the way. An employer closes shop.

Debt Increasing

Government, business and personal debt is exploding in our nation. If you converted the total debt to one-dollar bills, placed them end-to-end and pointed them out to space, they would extend more than a billion miles . . . beyond the sun! The economy is riding on a growing mountain of debt.

> . . . *free from the dominion of vice; by the practice of industry and frugality, free from debt, which exposes a man to confinement, and slavery to his creditors.*
>
> Benjamin Franklin, Eighteenth century

"With so much credit around you're bound to have casualties," Vern Countryman, a Harvard professor, explains. "It's just like auto accidents. If you're going to have all those cars, you're going to have accidents." In a recent year more than 850,000 individuals filed bankruptcy—more bankruptcies than during the Great Depression. Consumers now spend approximately one out of every five dollars in take-home pay on personal debts, not including the home mortgage. More sobering is a Gallup Poll that found 56 percent of all divorces are a result of financial tension in the home. For many, the more accurate marriage vow would have been "till debt do us part." Such financial tension exists largely because consumers believe the "gospel according to Madison Avenue," which says, "Buy now and pay later with *easy monthly payments*." We all know that nothing about those monthly payments is easy.

What Is Debt?

Lenders and advertisers use attractive definitions of debt that mask its harsh reality. The *Roget's College Thesaurus* lists the following synonyms for debt: liable, minus, owing, in hock, up against it, encumbered, insolvent, in the hole, broke. Do you feel uncomfortable as you read this list? I have yet to see one ad that promises the good life of "buy now and pay later" balanced with these words that describe the reality of debt. Are you beginning to have the feeling that the "gospel according to Madison Avenue" might not be preaching the whole truth of the abundant life as a member of the "debt set"?

> *Just as the rich rule the poor, so the borrower is servant to the lender.*
> KING SOLOMON,
> TENTH CENTURY, B.C.

The dictionary defines debt as "money or property which one person is obligated to pay to another." Debt includes money owed to credit-card companies, bank loans, money borrowed from relatives, the home mortgage and past due medical bills. Bills that come due, such as the monthly electric bill, are not considered debt if they are paid on time.

WHAT DOES DEBT REALLY COST?

We need to understand the real cost of debt. Two common types of debt are credit-card debt and the home mortgage.

Credit-Card Debt

Assume you have $5,560 in credit-card debt at an 18 percent interest rate. This would cost you about $1,000 in interest annually. Study the chart on page 36.

You can see what lenders have known for a long time — compounding interest has an incredible impact. It can work for you, or it can work against you. Assuming that the interest earned or spent has no tax consequences, if you pay a lender $1,000 each year for 40 years, he will accumulate $4,163,213 if he earns 18 percent on your payment. Is there any wonder credit-card companies are eager for you to become one of their borrowers?

Now compare the $40,000 you paid in interest during 40 years with the $767,091 you could have accumulated if you had invested $1,000 each year earning 12 percent. Clearly, debt has a much higher cost than many realize. Next time you are tempted to borrow, ask yourself if the long-term benefits of staying out of debt outweigh the short-term benefits of the purchase.

1. Amount of interest you paid:

Year 5	Year 10	Year 20	Year 30	Year 40
$5,000	$10,000	$20,000	$30,000	$40,000

2. What you would earn on the $1,000 invested at 12 percent:

Year 5	Year 10	Year 20	Year 30	Year 40
6,353	17,549	72,052	241,333	767,091

3. How much the lender earns from your payment at 18 percent:

Year 5	Year 10	Year 20	Year 30	Year 40
7,154	23,521	146,628	790,948	4,163,213

Home Mortgage

A 30-year home mortgage, at a 10 percent interest rate, will require you to pay more than three times the amount originally borrowed.

Original mortgage amount	$100,000.00
Monthly mortgage payment at 10 percent interest	$877.57
Months paid	x 360
Total payments	$315,925.20

Debt also extracts a physical toll. It often increases stress, which contributes to mental, physical and emotional fatigue. It can stifle creativity and harm relationships. Many people raise their standard of living through debt, only to discover that the burden of debt controls their lifestyles. The bumper sticker that reads, "I owe, I owe, it's off to work I go," is an unfortunate reality for too many people.

What Does Scripture Say About Debt?

Scripture's perspective on debt is clear. Read the first portion of Romans 13:8 carefully from several different Bible translations:

"Owe no man any thing" (KJV). "Pay all your debts" (LB). "Owe nothing to anyone." "Keep out of debt and owe no man anything" (AMP).

In Proverbs 22:7 we learn why our Lord speaks so directly to the area of debt: "Just as the rich rule the poor, so the borrower is servant to the lender" (LB). When we are in debt, we are in a position of servitude to the lender. Indeed, the deeper we are in debt, the more of a servant we become. We do not have the full freedom or discretion to decide where to spend our income because we have legally obligated ourselves to meet these debts.

In 1 Corinthians 7:23 Paul writes, "You were bought with a price; do not become slaves of men." Our Father made the ultimate sacrifice by giving His Son, the Lord Jesus Christ, to die for us. He now wants His children free to serve Him in whatever way He chooses.

Debt Considered a Curse
In the Old Testament one of the rewards for obedience was being out of debt. "Now it shall be, if you will diligently obey the Lord your God, being careful to do all His commandments which I command you today, the Lord your God will set you high above all the nations of the earth. And all these blessings shall come upon you and overtake you, if you will obey the Lord your God . . . and you shall lend to many nations, *but you shall not borrow*" (Deuteronomy 28:1-2, 12, emphasis added).

Conversely, indebtedness was one of the curses inflicted for disobedience. "But it shall come about, if you will not obey the Lord your God, to observe to do all His commandments and His statutes with which I charge you today, that all these curses shall come upon you and overtake you. . . . The alien who is among you shall rise above you higher and higher, but you shall go down lower and lower. *He shall lend to you*, but you shall not lend to him; he shall be the head, and you shall be the tail" (Deuteronomy 28:15, 43-44, emphasis added).

Debt Presumes Upon Tomorrow
When we get into debt, we assume that we will earn enough or will have sufficient resources to pay the debt. We plan for our job to continue or our business or investments to be profitable. Scripture

cautions us against presumption: "Come now, you who say, 'Today or tomorrow, we shall go to such and such a city, and spend a year there and engage in business and make a profit.' Yet you do not know what your life will be like tomorrow. You are just a vapor that appears for a little while and then vanishes away. Instead, you ought to say, 'If the Lord wills, we shall live and also do this or that'" (James 4:13-15).

Debt May Deny God an Opportunity

Financial author Ron Blue tells of a young man who wanted to go to seminary to become a missionary. The young man had no money and thought the only way he could afford seminary was to secure a student loan. However, this would have encumbered him with thousands of dollars of debt by the time he graduated. This would have been an impossible situation. He could not pay back his loan on a missionary's salary.

After a great deal of prayer, he decided to enroll without the help of a student loan and to trust the Lord to meet his needs. He graduated without borrowing anything and grew in his appreciation for how the sovereign, living God could creatively provide for his needs. This was the most valuable lesson learned in seminary. It prepared him for the mission field where he repeatedly depended on the Lord to meet his needs. Borrowing may deny God an opportunity to demonstrate His reality.

WHEN CAN WE OWE MONEY?

Scripture is silent on the subject of when we can owe money. In my opinion it is possible to owe money for a home mortgage or for your business or vocation. This "possible debt" is permissible, we believe, only if the following three criteria are met:

1. The item purchased is an asset with the potential to appreciate or to produce an income.
2. The value of the item equals or exceeds the amount owed against it.
3. The debt is not so large that repayment puts undue strain on the budget.

Let me give you an example of how a home mortgage might qualify. Historically, the home has usually been an appreciating asset; therefore, it meets the first criterion. Second, if you invest a reasonable down payment, you could expect to sell the home for at least enough to satisfy the mortgage, and this meets the second requirement. Third, the monthly house payment should not strain your budget.

If you meet all the criteria and assume some "possible debt," I hope you will immediately establish the goal of eliminating even it. We do not know if the housing market will appreciate or even maintain current values. Moreover, the loss of a job can interrupt your income. Therefore, I urge you to consider prayerfully paying off all debt.

GETTING OUT OF DEBT—
"D" DAY

W E HAVE SO MUCH personal debt in our nation that the average person has been described as someone driving on a bond-financed highway, in a bank-financed car, fueled by charge-card-financed gasoline, going to purchase furniture on the installment plan to put in his savings-and-loan-financed home!

"I hope I never pick up another one," Allen said.

"I just didn't know," Jean recalled. "I had no experience."

What were they talking about? Poisonous reptiles? Radioactive material? Hard drugs?

No. Credit cards. The Hitchcocks had run up thousands of dollars of debt on credit cards and were paying a high rate of interest for that "privilege." This is a common predicament. The easy availability of credit has spawned a phenomenal growth in the number of cards held by customers. People hold hundreds of millions of cards, and the average consumer packs away more than five cards in his wallet.

At the end of the initial conference with the Hitchcocks, Allen asked for my scissors. He wanted to perform some "plastic surgery." As a symbol of their vow to get out of debt, he cut their credit cards to ribbons. If they follow through in their commitment, they will be in the minority. Less than 50 percent of those who take the initial step actually follow through on their commitment and become debt-free.

How to Get Out of Debt

Because of your particular circumstances, your path for getting out of debt will be unique to you. The following 10 steps are a guide for your journey. The steps are simple, but following them requires hard work. The goal is "D" Day—Debtless Day, the day when you become absolutely free of debt.

1. Pray.

In 2 Kings 4:1-7 a widow was threatened with losing her children to her creditor, and she appealed to Elisha for help. Elisha instructed the widow to borrow many empty jars from her neighbors. The Lord supernaturally multiplied her only possession, a small quantity of oil, and as a result, all the jars were filled. She sold the oil and paid her debts to free her children. The same God who provided supernaturally for the widow is interested in you becoming free of debt as well.

The first step is the most important. Pray. Ask for the Lord's help and guidance in your journey toward Debtless Day. He might act immediately, as in the case of the widow, or slowly over time. In either case, prayer is essential.

I have observed a trend. As people begin to eliminate debt and accelerate debt repayment, the Lord blesses their faithfulness. Even if you can afford only a small monthly prepayment to reduce your debt, please do it. The Lord can multiply your efforts.

2. Establish a written budget.

In my experience, few people in debt have been using a written budget. They may have had one, neatly filed away in a drawer, but they have not been using it. A written budget helps you plan ahead and analyze your spending patterns to see where you can cut back. It is an effective bridle on impulse spending.

3. List your assets—everything you own.

List every possession you own: your home, car, furniture, etc. Evaluate the completed list to determine whether you should sell any assets. As we began to consider items the Hitchcocks might sell, the most obvious one was their new second car.

"I can't do without my car, Allen," Jean protested.

Allen looked hurt and guilty. He didn't want to deprive his wife of anything she wanted, but they both realized that drastic action was necessary. By deciding to sell the car and Allen's gun collection, the Hitchcocks cut their indebtedness and began to use the amount of the car payment to reduce some of their other debts.

There is an important lesson in what they did. They had to change their perspective on their possessions. As George Fooshee has said, "Your attitude toward things will determine your success in working your way out of debt. Don't think about how much you will lose or what you paid for the item you are selling. Think about how much you will gain which can be applied to your immediate debt reduction."[4]

4. List your liabilities—everything you owe.

Many people, particularly if they owe a lot of money, do not know exactly what they owe. However, you must list your debts to get an accurate picture of your current financial situation. You also need to list the interest rate your creditors are charging for each debt.

DEBT LIST—WHAT IS OWED

	Amount Owed	Monthly Payment	Interest Rate
Home mortgage	_____	_____	____
Credit card companies	_____	_____	____
Bank	_____	_____	____
Installment loans	_____	_____	____

(continued)

(continued from previous page)	Amount Owed	Monthly Payment	Interest Rate
Loan companies	_____	_____	____
Insurance companies	_____	_____	____
Credit union	_____	_____	____
Loans from relatives	_____	_____	____
Other personal loans	_____	_____	____
Business loans	_____	_____	____
Medical loans	_____	_____	____
Others	_____	_____	____
TOTAL DEBTS	_____	_____	

As you analyze the interest rates on your debt list, you will discover that credit costs vary greatly. Listing your debts will help you establish a priority of debt reduction.

5. Establish a debt repayment schedule for each creditor.
Again, getting out of debt may seem tedious, but it is absolutely necessary to follow these steps. Nobody ever gets out of debt by accident. We all need a systematic written payment schedule to reach the goal of "D" Day—"debtless day."

A typical repayment schedule looks like this:

Creditor: *Last National Bank*			
	Monthly Payment	Months Remaining	Balance Due
January	*100.00*	*12*	*1,150*
February	*100.00*	*11*	*1,061*
March	*100.00*	*10*	*970*

After you make your monthly payments, write down the amount paid and compute the balance due. This will give you a sense of accomplishment. It will enable you to watch the balance diminish, which will give you the incentive to persist in your plan.

If you are deeply in debt or have been past due on your payments to creditors, it is a good idea to send them a copy of your repayment schedule. It is the rare creditor who will not go along with a person making a serious effort to pay his or her debt. A creditor will appreciate the fact that you have made out a schedule and have been concerned enough to share it.

Decide which debts to pay off first. Your decision should be based on two factors: the size of the debts and the interest rate charged.

Pay off small debts. Focus on paying off the smallest debts first. You will be encouraged as they are eliminated, and this will free more cash to apply against other debts. After you pay off the first debt, apply its payment toward the next debt you wish to retire. After the second debt is paid off, apply what you were paying on the first and second debts toward the next debt you wish to eliminate and so forth.

Pay off higher interest rate debts. Note what rate of interest you are being charged on each debt and try to pay off those that charge the highest rate of interest before you pay off those that charge less.

6. Consider earning additional income.

Many people hold jobs that simply do not produce enough income to meet their needs even if they spend wisely. Two issues are important about earning additional income. First, decide in advance to pay off debts with the added earnings. We tend to spend more than we make, whether we earn much or little. Spending always seems to keep ahead of earning. Second, earn additional income without harming your relationship with the Lord or with your family. If you are married, you may need to be creative in finding ways to involve the whole family in a cottage industry or in finding a job that brings the family together rather than tearing it apart.

Jean Hitchcock proved to be an industrious and innovative person. She started a "mini-nursery" in her home, baby-sitting four children from her neighborhood during the day while the children's parents worked. The two older Hitchcock children were also encouraged to baby-sit in the evenings, and they contributed half of their earnings to the family's debt reduction.

These are only some of hundreds of imaginative ways to earn additional income to get out of debt more quickly. However, no matter how much additional income you earn, the key is a commitment that those moneys be applied to the reduction of debt and not to a higher level of spending.

7. Accumulate no new debt.
The only way I know to accumulate no additional debt is to pay for everything with cash, a check or a debit card at the time of purchase. This raises the issue of credit cards. I do not believe that credit cards are inherently sinful, but they are dangerous. Statistics show that people spend about one-third more when they use credit cards than when they use cash, because they feel they are not really spending money since they are using a plastic card. As one shopper said to another, "I like credit cards a lot more than money because they go so much further!"

When Bev and I began this study, we had nine credit cards. Today we carry one. When I analyze the financial situation of people in debt, I use a simple rule of thumb to determine whether credit cards are too dangerous for them. If they do not pay the entire balance due at the end of each month, I encourage them to perform plastic surgery. Any good scissors will do!

8. Be content with what you have.
We live in a culture whose advertising industry has devised powerful, sophisticated methods of persuading the consumer to buy. Frequently the message is intended to create discontentment with what we have.

An American company opened a new plant in Central America because labor was plentiful and inexpensive. The opening of the plant proceeded smoothly until the workers at the plant received their first paychecks. The next day none of the villagers reported for work. Management waited . . . one, two, three days. Still no villagers came to work. The plant manager went to see the village chief to talk about the problem. "Why should we continue to work?" the chief asked in response to the manager's inquiry. "We are satisfied. We have already earned all the money we need to live on."

The plant stood idle for two months until someone came up with the bright idea of sending a mail-order catalog to every villager. Reading the catalogs created new desires for the villagers. Soon they returned to work, and there has been no employment problem since then.

Note these three facts:

- The more television you watch, the more you spend.
- The more you look at catalogs and magazines, the more you spend.
- The more you shop, the more you spend.

Our family is evidence of this. When my daughter suddenly wants a special glass from a fast-food restaurant, I know she has seen a television commercial. Clearly, limiting our television viewing also limits our wants.

9. Consider a radical change in your lifestyle.
A growing number of people have lowered their expenses significantly to get out of debt more quickly. Some have sold their homes and moved to smaller ones or rented apartments or moved in with family members. Many have sold automobiles with large monthly payments and have purchased inexpensive used cars for cash. They have temporarily lowered their cost of living to become free from debt.

10. Do not give up!
Recognize from the beginning there will be a hundred reasons why you should quit or delay your efforts to get out of debt. Don't yield to the temptation of not following through on your commitment.

Don't stop until you have reached the marvelous goal of debt-free living. Remember, getting out of debt is just plain hard work, but the freedom is worth the struggle.

How Do We Escape the Auto Debt Trap?

Automobile debt is one of the leading causes of consumer indebtedness. About 70 percent of all the automobiles in our nation are financed. The average person keeps his car between three and four years. The average car lasts 10 years.

Here is how you can escape the auto debt trap. First, decide in advance to keep your car for at least six years. Second, pay off your automobile loan. Third, continue paying the monthly car payment but into your own savings account. Then, when you are ready to replace your car, the saved cash plus the trade-in should be sufficient to buy a good, low-mileage used car without going into debt.

What About the Home Mortgage?

I would like to challenge you to seek the Lord's direction concerning your home mortgage if you own a home. Is it possible that He may want you to pay off everything you owe, including your mortgage? Usually this is a long-term goal because of the size of the average mortgage.

When Bev and I began to explore seriously what God wanted for us, we sensed we were to work to pay off everything, including the mortgage. Frankly, this was an unrealistic goal for us at the time, but we researched how we might accomplish this.

Let's examine the payment schedule for a home mortgage. Please do not let the size of the mortgage or the rate of interest hinder your thinking. In the chart that follows we are assuming a $75,000 mortgage at a 12 percent interest rate. It is to be paid over 30 years. The first year of the payment schedule (also known as an amortization schedule) would look like the following chart.

As you can see, during the early years of the mortgage almost all the payments go to pay the interest. Of a total $9,257.64 in house payments made during the first year, only $272.26 went toward principal reduction. In fact, it will be 23½ years before the principal and the interest portions of the payment equal each other. I don't know about you, but a 30-year goal to pay off my home mortgage doesn't excite me. If this can be reduced to 15 years, then the goal becomes more attainable. There are several ways to pay off the mortgage in half the time.

Payment#	Month	Payment	Interest	Principal	Principal Balance
1	Jan	771.47	750.00	21.47	74,978.53
2	Feb	771.47	749.79	21.68	74,956.85
3	Mar	771.47	749.57	21.90	74,934.95
4	Apr	771.47	749.35	22.12	74,912.83
5	May	771.47	749.13	22.34	74,890.49
6	June	771.47	748.90	22.57	74,867.92
7	July	771.47	748.68	22.79	74,845.13
8	Aug	771.47	748.45	23.02	74,822.11
9	Sep	771.47	748.22	23.25	74,798.86
10	Oct	771.47	747.99	23.48	74,775.38
11	Nov	771.47	747.78	23.69	74,751.74
12	Dec	771.47	747.52	23.95	74,727.74
Totals for year:		9,257.64	8,985.38	272.26	

One method is to increase the amount of your monthly payment. In our example, a $75,000 mortgage at 12 percent interest payable over 30 years requires a monthly installment of $771.47. If you increase the monthly payment by $128.70 to $900.17, the mortgage will be fully paid in 15 years. During the 15 years you will have paid an additional $23,166 and will have saved $138,864 in interest during the life of your mortgage.

A second method is to prepay the next month's principal payment in addition to your regular monthly payment of $771.47. By doing this consistently for 15 years you will have paid off the entire mortgage. During the early years, the additional payment is low, but in the later years the extra payment will become substantial.

Examine your mortgage to make certain that the mortgage may be prepaid without any penalty. A home mortgage usually allows such prepayment. Let your lender know what you are planning. Not many borrowers prepay their mortgages, so he may be in shock for a while.

For Bev and me, this turned into an exciting time as we began to pay off our mortgage. The Lord provided additional funds in an unexpected way, and today we do not owe anyone anything. Elimination of debt allowed me to take time off from my work to study and develop Crown Ministries materials. Our living costs are more modest now, because we do not have any debts or house payments. God may have something similar in mind for you.

Investment Debt

Should you borrow money to make an investment? I believe it is permissible, but only if you are not personally required to guarantee the repayment of the debt. The investment for which you borrow and any money invested should be the sole collateral for the debt.

There is the possibility of difficult or catastrophic financial events over which you have no control. It is painful to lose your investment, but it is much more serious to jeopardize meeting your needs by risking all your assets on investment debt. This position may appear too conservative; however, many people have lost everything by guaranteeing debt on investments that went sour.

Business and Church Debt

I also want to encourage you to pray about becoming debt-free in your business and church. Many are beginning to pay off all business-related debts, and scores of churches are aggressively working toward satisfying their debts.

Debt Repayment Responsibilities

Some people delay payments in order to use the creditor's money as long as possible. There are seminars that actually teach people to live on the "ragged edge of being a dead beat," but this is not biblical. Proverbs 3:27-28 reads, "Do not withhold good from those to whom it is due, when it is in your power to do it. Do not say to your neighbor, 'Go, and come back, and tomorrow I will give it,' when you have it with you." Godly people should pay their debts and bills as promptly as they can. We have a policy of trying to pay each bill the same day we receive it to demonstrate to others that knowing Jesus Christ has made us financially responsible.

Should You Use All Your Savings to Pay Off Debt?

In my opinion it is wise not to deplete all your savings to pay off debt. Maintain a reasonable level of savings to provide for the unexpected. If you apply all your savings against debt and the unexpected does occur, you probably will be forced to incur more debt to fund the emergency.

Bankruptcy

In bankruptcy, a court of law declares a person unable to pay his debts. Depending upon the type of bankruptcy, the court will either allow the debtor to develop a plan to repay his creditors, or the court will distribute his property among the creditors as payment for the debts.

An epidemic of bankruptcy is sweeping our nation. Should a godly person declare bankruptcy? The answer is generally no. Psalm 37:21 tells us, "The wicked borrows and does not pay back, but the righteous is gracious and gives." However, in my opinion, bankruptcy is permissible under two circumstances: a creditor forces a person into bankruptcy, or a counselor believes the debtor's emotional health is at stake because of inability to cope with the pressure of unreasonable creditors. For example, if a husband deserts his wife and children, leaving her with business and family debts for which she is responsible, she may not have the resources or income to meet those obligations. The emotional trauma of an unwanted divorce, coupled with harassment from unsympathetic creditors, may be too much for her to bear.

After a person goes through bankruptcy, he should seek counsel from a competent attorney to determine if it's legally permissible to repay the debt, even though he is not obligated to do so. If it is allowable, he should make every effort to repay the debt. For a large debt, this may be a long-term goal that is largely dependent upon the Lord supernaturally providing the resources.

Co-Signing

Related to debt is the matter of co-signing. A person who co-signs becomes legally responsible for the debt of another. It is just as if you went to the bank, borrowed the money and gave it to your friend or relative who is asking you to co-sign.

A study by the Federal Trade Commission found that 50 percent of those who co-signed for bank loans ended up making payments. Seventy-five percent of those who co-signed for finance company loans ended up making payments. Unfortunately, few co-signers plan for default. The casualty rate is so high because the professional lender has analyzed the loan and said to himself, *I won't touch this with a 10-foot pole unless I can get someone who is financially responsible to guarantee this loan.*

Fortunately, Scripture speaks very clearly about co-signing. Proverbs 17:18 reads, "It is poor judgment to cosign another's note, to become responsible for his debts" (LB). The words *poor judgment* are better translated *"destitute of mind."*

A parent often co-signs for his or her child's first automobile, but we have decided not to do this. We want to model for our children the importance of not co-signing, and we also want to discourage them from using debt. Instead, we are training them to plan ahead and save for the cash purchase of their first car.

I urge you to use sound judgment and *never co-sign* a note or become surety for any debt.

If you have co-signed, Scripture gives you very direct counsel. Proverbs 6:1-5 reads,

> Son, if you endorse a note for someone you hardly know, guaranteeing his debt, you are in serious trouble. You may have trapped yourself by your agreement. Quick! Get out of it if you possibly can! Swallow your pride; don't let embarrassment stand in the way. Go and beg to have your name

erased. Don't put if off . . . if you can get out of this trap you have saved yourself like a deer that escapes from a hunter, or a bird from the net (LB).

CONTRAST

Society says: You may use debt as often as you wish; buy now and pay later.

Scripture says: The Lord discourages the use of debt because He wants us free to serve Him.

COMMITMENT

Formalize your desire to get out of debt. Then follow the 10 steps to becoming debt-free. Seek the help and counsel of some friends who can hold you accountable to stick to your plan.

The value of seeking advice is the subject of the next chapter.

COUNSEL—
A TRIPLE-BRAIDED CORD

JEAN AND ALLEN were faced with an uncomfortable decision. Jean's brother and his wife had just moved to Florida from Chicago. Because they experienced financial difficulties in Chicago, the bank would not loan them the money to purchase a home unless they had someone to co-sign the note. They asked Allen and Jean to co-sign. Jean pleaded for Allen to do so; however, he was reluctant.

> Two can accomplish more than twice as much as one.
> ECCLESIASTES 4:9, LB

When they came asking for advice to resolve this problem, I asked them to read the verses from the Bible that addressed co-signing. When Jean read the passages she responded, "Who am I to argue with God? We shouldn't co-sign." Allen was relieved.

Two years later, Jean's brother and his wife were divorced and he declared bankruptcy. Can you imagine the strain on their marriage if they had co-signed that note? They would not have been able to survive financially.

Fortunately, they sought counsel. This is a sharp contrast to our culture's practice that says, be a rugged individualist who makes decisions alone and unafraid, coping with any financial pressure in stoic silence.

King Solomon dominated the world scene in his time. Known as "the first great commercial king of Israel," he was a skilled diplomat and director of extensive building, shipping and mining ventures. However, Solomon is most often remembered as the wisest king who ever lived. In fact, he made wisdom a subject of study. In Proverbs he wrote, "Wisdom is better than jewels; and all desirable things cannot compare with her" (8:11). Solomon's practical recommendations for embracing wisdom are also found in Proverbs: "Listen to advice and accept instruction, and in the end you will be wise" (19:20, NIV). "The way of a fool is right in his own eyes, but a wise man is he who listens to counsel" (12:15).

Where Should We Seek Counsel?

The Bible encourages us to seek counsel from several sources.

Scripture

The psalmist wrote, "Your laws are both my light and my counselors" (Psalm 119:24, LB). Moreover, the Bible makes this remarkable claim about itself: "For the word of God is living and active and sharper than any two-edged sword . . . and able to judge the thoughts and intentions of the heart" (Hebrews 4:12). I have found this to be true. The Bible is a living book that our Lord uses to communicate His direction and truths to all generations. It is the first filter through which I put a financial decision. If the Scriptures clearly answer my question, I do not have to go any further because it contains the Lord's written, revealed will. If the Bible is not specific about a particular issue, I subject my decision to the second source of counsel: godly people.

Godly People

"The godly man is a good counselor because he is just and fair and knows right from wrong" (Psalm 37:30-31, LB). The apostle Paul recognized the benefit of godly counsel. After he was converted on the Damascus road, he never was alone in his public ministry. He knew and appreciated the value of a couple of extra sets of eyes looking down that straight and narrow road. Timothy, Barnabas, Luke or someone else was always with him.

In fact, in the New Testament *saint* is never used in the singular. It is always in the plural. Someone has described the Christian life as not one of independence from each other but of dependence upon each other. Nowhere is this more clearly illustrated than in Paul's discussion concerning the body of Christ in the 12th chapter of 1 Corinthians. Each of us is pictured as a different part of this body. Our ability to function effectively is dependent upon members working together. In other words, to operate in an optimum way, we need other people to help us. God has given each individual certain abilities and gifts, but God has not given any one person all the skills he or she needs to be most productive.

> *And one standing alone can be attacked and defeated, but two can stand back-to-back and conquer; three is even better, for a triple-braided cord is not easily broken.*
> ECCLESIASTES 4:12, LB

1. Spouse. If you are married, your spouse is to be your primary source of human counsel. A husband and wife are one. Women tend to be gifted with a wonderfully sensitive and intuitive nature that usually is very accurate. Men tend to focus objectively on the facts. A husband and wife need each other to achieve the proper balance for a correct decision. I also believe the Lord honors a wife's "office" as helpmate to her husband. Many times the Lord communicates most clearly to a husband through his wife.

Husbands, let me be blunt. Regardless of her business background or her financial aptitude, you must cultivate and seek your wife's counsel. I have done this, and it has been a pleasant surprise for me to observe how astute Bev's analysis has been concerning finances. Even though her formal education was not related to business, she has developed excellent business sense, and her decisions are often better than mine. Indeed, her perspective always enriches mine.

By consistently asking for her advice, you keep your wife informed of your true financial condition. This is important in the event a husband dies before his wife or if he is unable to work. My father suffered a massive heart attack that incapacitated him for two years. Because he had been faithful in keeping my mother abreast of his business, she was able to step in and operate it successfully.

Seeking the counsel of your spouse also helps preserve your relationship because you will both experience the consequences of a decision. If you both agree about a decision, even if it proves to be disastrous, your relationship is more likely to remain intact.

2. Parents. We should seek counsel of our parents also. Proverbs 6:20-22 says, "My son, observe the commandment of your father, and do not forsake the teaching of your mother . . . When you walk about, they will guide you." I cannot tell you how much I have benefited from the counsel of my father and mother. Our parents have the benefit of years of experience. They know us so very well, and they have our best interests at heart.

In my opinion we should seek their counsel even if they do not yet know Christ or have not been faithful money managers themselves. It is not uncommon for an unspoken barrier to be erected between a child and his parents. Asking their advice is a way to honor them and to build a bridge across any wall.

A word of caution: Genesis 2:24 reads, "A man shall leave his father and his mother, and shall cleave to his wife; and they shall become one flesh." Although a husband and wife should seek the counsel of their parents, the advice of the parents should be subordinate to the advice of a spouse, especially if a family conflict materializes.

The Lord.
During the process of searching the Bible and obtaining the counsel of godly people, we need to ask the Lord for direction. In Isaiah 9:6 we are told that one of the Lord's names is "Wonderful Counselor." The Psalms clearly identify the Lord as our counselor. "I [the Lord] will instruct you and teach you in the way which you should go; I will counsel you with My eye upon you" (Psalm 32:8). "I will bless the Lord who has counseled me" (Psalm 16:7).

We receive the counsel of the Lord by praying and listening. Tell the Lord about your concerns and need for specific direction. Then quietly listen for His still, small voice.

A MULTITUDE OF COUNSELORS

We should try to obtain advice from a multitude of counselors. Proverbs 15:22 reads, "Plans fail for lack of counsel, but with many advisers they succeed" (NIV). And Proverbs 11:14 says, "Where there is no guidance, the people fall, but in abundance of counselors there is victory."

The older I have become and the larger Crown Ministries has grown, the more I recognize my need for a multitude of counselors. Each of us has a limited range of knowledge and experience, and we need others, with their own unique backgrounds, to give us insights and alternatives we never would have considered without their advice. One of the Lord's most gracious gifts to me has been surrounding me with a wise board of directors and an unusually competent team of staff members whose counsel has been invaluable.

Another practical way of applying the principle of many counselors is to become involved in a small group. For years I have met regularly with a small group to pray and share. Through the years our group has been through traumatic times together. New-born babies, deaths of parents, job changes, starting new businesses, home and car purchases and financial pressures have marked the years. The advice of these friends has not only benefited our checkbook but has significantly contributed to our emotional and spiritual health. We have rejoiced together during each other's successes. We have comforted and wept with each other during the difficult times.

We have learned that when someone is subjected to a painful circumstance, it is difficult for him or her to make wise, objective decisions. We have experienced the safety of having a group of people who love one another—even when it hurts. I am more receptive to constructive criticism when it comes from someone I respect, someone who cares for me. Solomon describes the benefits of dependence upon one another in one of my favorite passages:

> Two are better than one because they have a good return for their labor. For if either of them falls, the one will lift up his

companion. But woe to the one who falls when there is not another to lift him up . . . And if one can overpower him who is alone, two can resist him. A cord of three strands is not quickly torn apart (Ecclesiastes 4:9-12).

Big Decisions

Because of their importance and permanence, some decisions deserve more attention than others. Decisions concerning a career or a home purchase, for example, affect us for a longer period of time than most other choices we make. Throughout Scripture we are admonished to wait upon the Lord. Whenever you face a major decision or experience a sense of confusion concerning a course of action, I encourage you to set aside some time to pray, fast and listen quietly for His will.

COUNSEL TO BE AVOIDED

We need to avoid one particular source of counsel. "How blessed is the man who does not walk in the counsel of the wicked" (Psalm 1:1). The word "blessed" literally means "happy many times over." A "wicked" person is one who lives his life without regard to God. In my opinion, we can seek specific technical assistance, such as legal and accounting advice, from those who do not know God. Then armed with the technical data, our final decision should be based on the counsel of those who know the Lord.

Never Seek the Counsel of Fortune Tellers or Mediums

The Bible bluntly tells us never to seek the advice of fortune tellers, mediums or spiritualists: "Do not turn to mediums or spiritists; do not seek them out to be defiled by them. I am the Lord your God" (Leviticus 19:31). Study this next passage carefully: "So Saul died for his trespass which he committed against the Lord . . . and also because he asked counsel of a medium, making inquiry of it, and did not inquire of the Lord. Therefore He killed him" (1 Chronicles 10:13-14). Saul died, in part, because he went to a medium. We should also avoid any methods they use in forecasting the future, such as horoscopes, Ouija boards and all other practices of the occult.

Be Careful of the Biased

We need to be cautious of the counsel of the biased. When receiving financial advice, ask yourself this question: *What stake does this person have in the outcome of my decision?* If the adviser will profit, always seek a second unbiased opinion.

CONTRAST

Society says: Be your own person; stand on your own two feet. You don't need anyone to tell you what to do.

Scripture says: "The wise man is glad to be instructed, but a self-sufficient fool falls flat on his face" (Proverbs 10:8, LB).

COMMITMENT

In my experience, the vast majority of those in financial difficulties have not followed the scriptural principle of seeking wise counsel. They have been molded by our culture's view that admitting a need and asking for advice is only for those who are not strong enough to be self-sufficient.

More often than not, a person's pride is the biggest deterrent to seeking advice. This is especially true in a financial crisis. It is embarrassing to expose our problems to someone else.

Another reason for reluctance to seek counsel is the fear that an objective evaluation of our finances may bring to the surface issues we would rather avoid: a lack of disciplined spending, an unrealistic budget, a lack of communication in the family or a suggestion to give up something dear to us.

I cannot overemphasize the importance of counsel, and I encourage you to evaluate your situation. If you do not have a counselor, try to cultivate a friendship with at least one godly person who can advise you.

HONESTY—
ABSOLUTELY

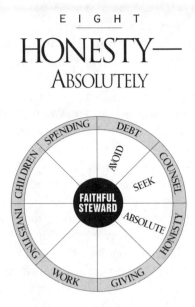

ONE EVENING I received a phone call I will never forget. It was from Allen Hitchock. "You won't believe what just happened to me!" he said. "I went to my local gas station and pumped $10 worth of gas. When I asked for a receipt, the attendant made the receipt for $15. When I pointed out this mistake, the attendant replied, 'Oh, just turn in the receipt to your company, and you'll make a fast five bucks. After all, a lot of the mailmen do that.'"

> *Every man did what was right in his own eyes.*
> JUDGES 17:6

Like Allen, all of us—the executive, the employee and the homemaker—have to make daily decisions about whether or not to handle money honestly. Do you tell the cashier at the grocery store when you receive too much change? Have you ever tried to sell something and been tempted not to tell the whole truth because you might lose a sale?

HONESTY IN SOCIETY

These decisions are made more difficult because everyone around us seems to be dishonest. For example, employee theft in the workplace is approaching $1 billion a week.

Byron was reading the morning paper while his wife, Peggy, prepared breakfast. "Well, would you look at this. Another politician got caught with his hand in the cookie jar," he said. "I'll bet there isn't an honest one in the entire country. What a bunch of crooks!"

Just a few moments later Byron was smirking as he told Peggy how he planned to pad his expense account in such a way that he would get more money from his employer than he was entitled to receive. Byron was not aware of the incongruity between his own behavior and his disgust with dishonesty in others. As he told Peggy, "The way the economy is going, you've got to be shrewd just to survive. The company doesn't need it, and besides, everyone does it."

We live in an age of "relative honesty" in which people formulate their own standards of honesty which change with the circumstances. The Bible speaks of a similar time which was a turbulent period in Israel's history. "Everyone did whatever he wanted to—whatever seemed right in his own eyes" (Judges 17:6, LB).

HONESTY IN SCRIPTURE

Relative honesty contrasts sharply with the standard we find in Scripture. God demands absolute honesty. Proverbs 20:23 reads, "The Lord loathes all cheating and dishonesty" (LB). And Proverbs 12 :22 states, "Lying lips are an abomination to the Lord." Leviticus 19:11 says, "You shall not steal, nor deal falsely, nor lie to one another."

Study this comparison between what the Scriptures teach and what our society practices concerning honesty.

ISSUE	SCRIPTURE	SOCIETY
Standard of honesty	Absolute	Relative
God's concern about honesty	He demands honesty	There is no God
The decision to be honest or dishonest is based upon	Faith in the invisible, living God	Only the facts that can be seen
Question usually asked deciding whether to be honest	Will it please God?	Will I get away with it?

The God of Truth

Truthfulness is one of God's attributes. "I am . . . the truth" (John 14:6). Moreover, He commands us to reflect His honest and holy character: "Be holy yourselves also in all your behavior; because it is written, 'You shall be holy, for I am holy'" (1 Peter 1:15-16).

God's nature is in stark contrast to Satan's nature. John 8:44 describes the devil's character: "[The devil] . . . does not stand in the truth, because there is no truth in him. Whenever he speaks a lie, he speaks from his own nature; for he is a liar, and the father of lies." The Lord wants us to become conformed to His honest character rather than to the dishonest nature of the devil.

WHY DOES GOD DEMAND ABSOLUTE HONESTY?

God has imposed the standard of absolute honesty for five reasons.

1. We cannot practice dishonesty and love God.

When we practice dishonesty, we are acting as if the living God does not exist, and it is impossible to love God if He doesn't exist. Stop and think about what we are saying when we make a decision to be dishonest:

- God is not able to provide exactly what I need—even though He has promised to do so (Matthew 6:33). I will take things into my own hands and do them my own dishonest way.
- God is incapable of discovering my dishonesty.
- God is powerless to discipline me.

If we really believed that God would discipline us, then we would not consider acting dishonestly.

Honest behavior is an issue of faith. An honest decision may look foolish in light of the circumstances we can observe. However, a godly person has mastered the art of considering another factor which is valid, even though invisible: the person of Jesus Christ. Every honest decision strengthens our faith in the living God. However, if we choose to be dishonest, we essentially deny the existence of the Lord. Scripture declares that those who practice dishonesty hate God: "He who walks in his uprightness fears the Lord, but he who is crooked in his ways despises Him" (Proverbs 14:2).

2. We cannot practice dishonesty and love our neighbor.

The Lord demands absolute honesty because dishonest behavior violates the second commandment, "Thou shalt love thy neighbour as thyself" (Mark 12:31, KJV). Romans 13:9-10 reads, "If you love your neighbor as much as you love yourself you will not want to harm or cheat him . . . or steal from him . . . Love does no wrong to anyone" (LB).

When we act dishonestly, we are stealing from another person. We may fool ourselves into thinking it is a business or the government or an insurance company that is suffering loss, but if we look at the bottom line, it is the business owners or fellow taxpayers or policyholders from whom we are stealing. It is just as if we took the money from their wallets. We need to remember that dishonesty always injures people.

3. Honesty creates credibility for evangelism.

Our Lord demands that we be absolutely honest in order to demonstrate the reality of Jesus Christ to those who do not yet know Him. Our actions speak louder than our words. Scripture says to "prove yourselves to be blameless and innocent, children of God above reproach in the midst of a crooked and perverse generation, among whom you appear as lights in the world" (Philippians 2:15).

Robert Newsome had been trying to sell an old pickup truck for months. Finally, an interested buyer decided to purchase the truck, but at the last moment he told Newsome, "I'll buy the truck only if you don't report it to the state so I won't have to pay sales tax."

Newsome was tempted, but he knew it would be wrong. He responded, "I'm sorry, I can't do that because Jesus Christ is my Lord."

"You should have seen the buyer's face," Newsome said a few days later. "He almost went into shock. Then an interesting thing happened. He purchased the truck, and his attitude completely changed. He became very open to the truth of knowing Jesus Christ in a personal way." Honest behavior confirms to those who do not yet know Him that we serve a holy God.

4. Honesty confirms God's direction.

Proverbs 4:24-26 reads, "Put away from you a deceitful mouth, and put devious lips far from you. Let your eyes look directly ahead . . . Watch the path of your feet, and all your ways will be established."

What a tremendous principle! As you are absolutely honest, *"all your ways will be established."* Choosing to walk the narrow path of honesty eliminates the many possible avenues of dishonesty. Decision-making becomes simpler because the honest path is a clear path.

"If only I'd understood this," Raymond said as tears streamed down his cheeks.

"Donna and I wanted that house so much. It was our dream home, but our debts were so large that we couldn't qualify for the mortgage. The only way we could buy the house was to hide some of our debts from the bank. It was the worst decision of our lives. Almost immediately we were unable to meet the mortgage payment and pay our other debts too. The pressure built. It was almost more than Donna could stand. Our dream house ended up causing a family nightmare. I not only lost the home, but I nearly lost my wife."

Had Raymond and Donna been honest, the bank would not have approved the loan. They would not have been able to purchase that particular home. If they had prayed and waited, perhaps the Lord would have brought them something more affordable, thus avoiding the pressure that almost ended their marriage. Honesty helps confirm God's direction.

5. Even the small act of dishonesty is devastating.

God requires us to be *absolutely honest* because even the smallest act of dishonesty is sin. Even the smallest "white lie" can harden our hearts and make our consciences increasingly insensitive to sin. This can deafen our ears to the still, small voice of the Lord. A single cancer cell of small dishonesty can multiply and spread to greater dishonesty. "Whoever is dishonest with very little will also be dishonest with much" (Luke 16:10, NIV).

An event in Abraham's life has challenged me to be honest in small matters. The king of Sodom offered Abraham all the goods Abraham recovered when he returned from successfully rescuing the people of Sodom. Abraham answered the king, "I have sworn to the Lord . . . that I will not take a thread or a sandal thong or anything that is yours" (Genesis 14:22-23).

Just as Abraham was unwilling to take so much as a thread or a sandal thong, I challenge you to make a similar commitment in this area of honesty. Promise (or make a covenant) not to steal a stamp, or a photocopy, or a paper clip, or a long-distance telephone call, or a penny from your employer, the government or anyone else.

The people of God must be honest in even the smallest, seemingly inconsequential matters.

HOW DO WE ESCAPE THE TEMPTATION OF DISHONESTY?

Unless we deny ourselves and live our lives yielded to the Holy Spirit, all of us will be dishonest. "Live by the Spirit, and you will not gratify the desires of the sinful nature" (Galatians 5:16, NIV). The desire of our human nature is to act dishonestly. "Out of men's hearts, come evil thoughts . . . theft . . . deceit" (Mark 7:21-22, NIV). The desire of the Spirit is for us to be absolutely honest. I can't overemphasize that the life of absolute honesty is supernatural. We must submit ourselves entirely to Christ as Lord and allow Him to live His life through us. The most challenging book I have read on yielding to the Holy Spirit is *Humility* by Andrew Murray. I heartily recommend it to you.

By a Healthy Fear of the Lord
Proverbs 16:6 reads, "By the fear of the Lord one keeps away from evil." A "healthy fear" of the Lord does not mean that we have to view God as a big bully just waiting for the opportunity to punish us; rather, He is a loving Father who, out of infinite love, disciplines His children for their benefit. "He disciplines us for our good, that we may share His holiness" (Hebrews 12:10).

I once shared a motel room with a friend during a business trip. As we were leaving, he slipped one of the motel's drinking glasses into his pocket and walked to the car. Suddenly I was overwhelmed by the fear of the Lord. It is difficult to explain the feeling. The closest description I've found is in Daniel 5:6, which records the Babylonian king's reaction to the handwriting on the wall: "The king's . . . thoughts troubled him, so that the joints of his loins were loosed, and his knees smote one against another" (KJV).

There I was with my knees knocking as I thought of Hebrews 12:11, "All discipline for the moment seems not to be joyful, but sorrowful." Discipline hurts! Given the choice, I would rather *"share His holiness"* out of obedience to His Word than to make a deliberate decision that would prompt my loving Father to discipline me. I can't tell you how relieved I was when my friend returned the glass after I pleaded with him to do so!

By a Loss of Property
I believe that our heavenly Father will not allow us to keep anything we have acquired dishonestly. Proverbs 13:11 reads, "Wealth obtained by fraud dwindles."

Linda purchased four azalea plants, but the checkout clerk had only charged her for one. She knew it, but she left the store anyway without paying for the other three. She said it was simply miraculous how quickly three of those four plants died.

Think about this for a moment: If you are a parent and your child steals something, do you allow the child to keep it? Of course not. You require its return because the child's character would be damaged if he kept the stolen property. Not only do you insist upon its return, but you probably want the child to experience enough discomfort to produce a lasting impression. For example, you might have the child confess the theft and ask forgiveness from the store manager. When our heavenly Father lovingly disciplines us, it usually is done in such a way that we will not forget.

WHAT SHOULD WE DO WHEN WE HAVE BEEN DISHONEST?

Unfortunately, all of us are dishonest from time to time. Once we recognize that we have acted dishonestly, we need to do three things:

1. Restore our fellowship with God.

Anytime we sin, our fellowship with the Lord is broken. This needs to be restored. First John 1:9 tells us how: "If we confess our sins, He is faithful and righteous to forgive us our sins and to cleanse us from all unrighteousness." We must agree with God that our dishonesty is sin and then accept His gracious forgiveness so we can again enjoy His fellowship.

2. Restore our fellowship with people.

We need to confess our dishonesty to the person we offended. "Confess your sins to one another" (James 5:16). This has been difficult for me. After years of avoiding this step, I have started confessing my dishonesty to others. A person's lack of financial prosperity may be a consequence of violating this principle. "He who conceals his transgressions will not prosper, but he who confesses and forsakes them will find compassion" (Proverbs 28:13).

3. Restore any dishonestly acquired property.

If we have acquired anything dishonestly, we must return it to its rightful owner. "Then it shall be, when he sins and becomes guilty, that he shall restore what he took by robbery . . . or anything about which he swore falsely; he shall make restitution for it in full, and add to it one-fifth more. He shall give it to the one to whom it belongs" (Leviticus 6:4-5).

Restitution is a tangible expression of repentance and an effort to correct a wrong. If it's not possible for restitution to be made to the injured party, then the property should be given to the Lord. Numbers 5:8 teaches, "But if the man has no relative to whom restitution may be made for the wrong, the restitution . . . must go to the Lord for the priest."

BRIBES

A bribe is defined as anything given to a person to influence him to do something illegal or wrong. Taking a bribe is clearly prohibited by Scripture: "And you shall not take a bribe, for a bribe blinds the clear-sighted and subverts the cause of the just" (Exodus 23:8).

Bribes are sometimes subtly disguised as a "gift" or "referral fee." Evaluate any such offer to confirm that it is not in reality a bribe.

BLESSINGS AND CURSES

Listed below are some of the blessings the Lord has promised for the honest and some of the curses reserved for the dishonest. Read these slowly and prayerfully and ask God to use His Word to motivate you to a life of honesty.

Blessings Promised for the Honest

- **Intimacy with the Lord.** "For the crooked man is an abomination to the Lord; but He is intimate with the upright" (Proverbs 3:32).
- **A blessed family.** "A righteous man who walks in his integrity—how blessed are his sons after him" (Proverbs 20:7).
- **Long life.** "Truthful lips will be established forever, but a lying tongue is only for a moment" (Proverbs 12:19).
- **Prosperity.** "Much wealth is in the house of the righteous, but trouble is in the income of the wicked" (Proverbs 15:6).

Curses Reserved for the Dishonest

- **Alienation from God.** "For the crooked man is an abomination to the Lord" (Proverbs 3:32).
- **Family problems.** "He who profits illicitly troubles his own house" (Proverbs 15:27).
- **Death.** "The getting of treasures by a lying tongue is a fleeting vapor, the pursuit of death" (Proverbs 21:6).
- **Poverty.** "Wealth obtained by fraud dwindles" (Proverbs 13:11).

ARE YOU THE PERSON THE LORD IS LOOKING FOR?

I believe we seriously underestimate the impact that *one* honest person can have. Read Jeremiah 5:1 carefully, "Roam to and fro through the streets of Jerusalem, and look now, and take note . . . if you can find a man, if there is one who does justice, who seeks truth, then I [the Lord] will pardon her." The destiny of an entire city hung in the balance. Its future depended upon there being one absolutely honest person. Will you be that person for your community? You may not receive the acclaim of the media, the business community or politicians, but in God's economy, your commitment to honesty can have a massive influence on your city.

CONTRAST

Society says: You can be dishonest because everyone else is.

Scripture says: The Lord demands absolute honesty in even the smallest matters.

COMMITMENT

Prayerfully review this checklist for honest behavior:

1. Do I report all income on my tax returns, and are all my tax deductions legitimate?
2. Do I care for the property of others as if it were my own?
3. Do I have the habit of telling "little white lies"?
4. Do I ever misappropriate office supplies, stamps or anything else that belongs to my employer?
5. If I am undercharged on a purchase, do I report it?
6. Do I look out for the interests of others as well as my own?

Ask God to show you any other dishonest behavior that should be changed, especially in the gray areas. Ask a close friend to encourage you and to hold you accountable to be honest.

GIVING —
WHAT IS YOUR ATTITUDE?

A LLEN AND JEAN decided to enroll in a Crown Ministries small group study to learn what the Scriptures teach about money. A couple of months after the group started, I met Allen for breakfast. He told me how much the study meant to him, and then sheepishly confessed, "I've never had any desire to give money. Now that I understand what the Bible has to say about it, I want to give, but I'm frustrated. How can I possibly decide where to give? It seems as if my mailbox is constantly filled with appeals. There are so many needs. I feel guilty that perhaps we're not giving enough. And sometimes I become cynical because I feel I'm manipulated subtly by people whose goals may be worthwhile but whose means of achieving those goals are questionable."

> *It is more blessed to give than to receive.*
> JESUS CHRIST
> FROM ACTS 20:35

I knew what Allen was experiencing. I used to be as frustrated as he was. Since learning what Scripture says about giving, the Holy Spirit has been changing my attitudes, and I have experienced the blessings of giving. Indeed, giving has been the most liberating area in my Christian experience.

The Old and New Testaments place a great deal of emphasis on giving. In fact, there are more verses related to giving than any other subject on money. There are commands, practical suggestions, examples and exhortations concerning this facet of stewardship. Everywhere in the Bible covetousness and greed are condemned, and generosity and charity are encouraged.

Attitude in Giving

Giving with the proper attitude is crucial. First Corinthians 13:3 reads, "If I give all my possessions to feed the poor . . . but do not have love, it profits me nothing." It is hard to imagine anything more commendable than giving everything to the poor. But if it is done with the wrong attitude, without love, it is of no benefit to the giver. The Lord set the example of giving motivated by love. "For God so *loved* the world, that He *gave* His only begotten Son" (John 3:16, italics added). Note the sequence: Because God loved, He gave.

I struggled for years to give consistently out of a heart of love. I believe the only way to do this is to recognize that each gift is actually given to the Lord Himself. An example of this perspective is found in Numbers 18:24: "For the tithe of the sons of Israel, which they offer as an offering to the Lord, I have given to the Levites." If giving is merely to a church, a ministry or to a needy person, it is only charity. But if it is to the Lord, it becomes an act of worship. Because Jesus Christ is our Creator, our Savior and our faithful Provider, we can express our gratefulness and love by giving our gifts to Him. For example, when the offering plate is being passed at church, we should consciously remind ourselves that we are giving our gifts to the Lord Himself.

Stop and examine yourself. What is your attitude toward giving? I cannot stress too much the importance of giving with the proper attitude.

Advantages of Giving

Of course, a gift benefits the recipient, but according to God's economy, if a gift is given with the proper attitude, the giver benefits more than the receiver. "Remember the words of the Lord Jesus, that He Himself said, 'It is more blessed to give than to receive'" (Acts 20:35). As we examine Scripture, we find the giver benefits in four significant areas.

Increase in Intimacy

Above all else, giving directs our attention and hearts to Christ. Matthew 6:21 tells us, "For where your treasure is, there will your heart be also." This is why it is so necessary to go through the process of consciously giving each gift to the person of Jesus Christ. When you give your gift to Him, your heart will automatically be drawn to the Lord.

Development of Character

Our heavenly Father wants us as His children to be conformed to the image of His Son. The character of Christ is unselfish. Unfortunately, humans are by nature selfish. One of the key ways our character becomes conformed to Christ is by habitual giving. Someone once said, "Giving is not God's way of raising money; it is God's way of raising people into the likeness of His Son." The Lord understands that for us to develop into the people He wants us to be, we must learn how to share our possessions freely. If we don't, our inbred selfishness will grow and dominate us.

"An extreme example is Howard Hughes. In his youth Hughes was a typical playboy with a passion for parties and beautiful women and an aversion toward giving. As he grew older and turned an inheritance into a vast fortune, he became more and more closed-fisted. He let his wealth create an ever-increasing barrier between himself and other people. In his last years he lived in seclusion and became a recluse whose life was devoted to avoiding germs and people."[5]

George Mueller is a sharp contrast to Hughes. Mueller also inherited wealth, but unlike Hughes, he established a life-long pattern of generous sharing. His life was characterized by serving the needs of others. Sharing leads to life itself. It is the most effective antidote to the human disease of covetousness. "Instruct them . . . to be generous and ready to share . . . so that they may take hold of that which is life indeed" (1 Timothy 6:18-19).

Investments for Eternity

Matthew 6:20 reads, "But lay up for yourselves treasures in heaven, where neither moth nor rust destroys, and where thieves do not break in or steal." The Lord tells us that there really is something akin to the "First National Bank of Heaven." He wants us to know that we can invest for eternity.

Paul wrote, "Not that I seek the gift itself, but I seek for the profit which increases to your account" (Philippians 4:17). A literal account exists for each of us in heaven. We will be privileged to enjoy it forever. Scripture teaches that we "can't take it with us," but we can make deposits to our heavenly account before we die.

Randy Alcorn in his excellent book *Money, Possessions and Eternity,* illustrates the wisdom and value of eternal investments.

> Imagine for a moment that you are alive at the end of the Civil War. You are living in the South, but your home is really in the North. While in the South you have accumulated a good amount of Confederate currency. Suppose you know that the North is going to win the war soon. What will you do with your Confederate money?
>
> If you were smart, there is only one answer to the question. You would cash in your Confederate currency for U.S. currency—the only money that will have value once the war is over. You would keep only enough Confederate currency to meet your basic needs for that short period until the war was over.
>
> The currency of this world will be worthless at our death or at Christ's return, both of which are imminent. For us to accumulate vast earthly treasures in the face of the inevitable future is the equivalent to stockpiling Confederate money.
>
> The only currency of value in heaven is our present service and generous giving to God's kingdom. Jim Elliot, the martyred missionary, said it this way, "He is no fool who gives what he cannot keep to gain what he cannot lose."

Increase in Material Blessings

Giving with the proper attitude also results in a material increase flowing to the giver. Proverbs 11:24-25 reads, "There is one who scatters, yet increases all the more, and there is one who withholds what is justly due, but it results only in want. The generous man will be prosperous, and he who waters will himself be watered."

Examine 2 Corinthians 9:6-8: "He who sows bountifully shall also reap bountifully . . . God is able to make all grace abound to you, that . . . you may have an abundance for every good deed." These verses clearly teach that giving results in a material increase, but note carefully *why* the Lord returns an increase materially: *"that . . . you may have an abundance for every good deed."* As shown on the diagram below, the Lord produces an increase so that we may give more and have our needs met at the same time.

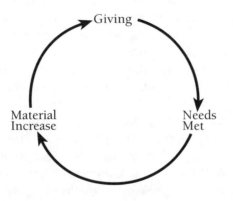

THE AMOUNT TO GIVE

Let's survey what the Scriptures say about how much to give. Under the Old Testament a tithe, or 10 percent of a person's earnings, was required to be given. When the children of Israel disobeyed this commandment, it was regarded as robbing God Himself. Listen to Jehovah's solemn words in Malachi's days: "You have robbed me of the tithes and offerings due to me. And so the awesome curse of God is cursing you, for your whole nation has been robbing me" (Malachi 3:8-9, LB).

In addition to the tithe, the Hebrews were to give offerings.

Furthermore, the Lord made special provisions for the needs of the poor. For example, every seven years all debts were forgiven, and special rules governed harvesting so that the poor could gather food.

In the New Testament the tithe is neither specifically rejected nor specifically recommended. It does teach us to give in proportion to the material blessing we have received, and it especially commends sacrificial giving.

What I like about the tithe or any fixed percentage of giving is that it is systematic, and the amount of the gift is easy to compute. The danger of the tithe is that it can be treated simply as another bill to be paid. By not giving out of a heart of love, I place myself in a position where I cannot receive the blessings the Lord has designed for a giver. Another potential danger of tithing is the view that once I have tithed, I have fulfilled all my obligations to give. For many Christians the tithe should be the beginning of their giving, not the limit.

Scripture is unclear on exactly how much we should give. I believe this lack of clarity is because the decision concerning the amount an individual gives should be based on a personal relationship with God. As we seek the guidance of the Spirit through an active prayer life, sharing suddenly becomes an exciting adventure.

The Abernathy family is an example. They used to own a shoe store. The members of the family had been praying that God would direct their sharing. As they prayed, they were impressed with the needs of the Wilsons, a large family in their community. Finances were tight for the Wilsons because the school year was starting. The Abernathys decided to give each of the five Wilson children two pairs of shoes. They did not know that the shoes had been precisely what the Wilson children had been praying for.

Around the dinner table one evening the Wilson children again prayed for shoes. After they were finished with their prayers, their mother said, "You don't have to ask the Lord for shoes anymore. God has answered your prayers." One by one the shoes were brought out.

By the time it was over, the children thought God was in the shoe business! I wish you could have seen the sense of awe on the faces of the Abernathys as they experienced firsthand how God was directing their sharing through the quiet mystery of prayer.

How much should you give?

To answer this question, first submit yourself to God. Earnestly seek His will for you.

Bev and I have given a great deal of thought and prayer to the question of how much we should share. We have concluded that the tithe is the minimum amount we should give. Then, we give over and above the tithe as God prospers or directs.

THE PATTERN OF GIVING

During Paul's third missionary journey he wrote the Corinthians concerning a promised collection to meet the needs of the persecuted believers in Jerusalem. "On the first day of every week let each one of you put aside and save, as he may prosper, that no collections be made when I come" (1 Corinthians 16:2). His comments provide practical instruction about giving. Let's call this pattern "Paul's Pod of P's," giving that is personal, periodic, private deposit and premeditated.

Giving should be *personal*.

Giving is the privilege and responsibility of every Christian, young and old, rich and poor. *"Let each one of you . . ."* The benefits of giving are intended for each person to enjoy.

Several years ago I met a neighbor who loved to give. It was immediately apparent to me that he gained great pleasure from giving. I had never met a person like that before. As our relationship has grown, I have discovered how he learned to be a joyful giver. His parents shared generously with those in need and required each of their children to establish this habit. As a consequence, he continues to enjoy a level of freedom in sharing that few people experience.

Giving should be *periodic*.

Periodic is the second of Paul's P's. The Lord understands that we need to give regularly, *"on the first day of every week."* Giving regularly helps draw us consistently to Christ.

Giving should be out of a *private deposit.*
"Put aside and save . . ." If you experience difficulty in monitoring the money you have decided to give, consider opening a separate checking account. Bev and I call ours the "Lord's account." You might also do something as simple as setting aside a special "cookie jar" into which you deposit the money you intend to give.

The most gratifying part of setting aside money has been the thrill of praying that God would make us aware of needs and then enable us to respond.

Giving should be *premeditated.*
Almost every Sunday after I became a Christian, Bev would ask me, "Honey, how much would you like to give this week at church?" My standard reply was, "I don't care. You make that decision." Because of my cavalier attitude, I was not in a position to experience the blessing meant for the giver. To know the full joy and reap the blessing of giving, it must not be done carelessly. "Let each one do just as he has purposed in his heart; not grudgingly or under compulsion; for God loves a cheerful giver" (2 Corinthians 9:7). Our giving should involve thought, planning and prayer. However, many believers operate like I used to—never thinking about giving until it is time for the collection.

The supreme example of premeditated giving was set by our Savior, "who for the joy set before Him endured the cross" (Hebrews 12:2).

TO WHOM DO WE GIVE?

We are told to share with three categories of people. With whom and in what proportion one gives varies with the needs God lays on the heart of each believer.

The Family
In our culture we are experiencing a tragic breakdown in this area of sharing. Husbands have failed to provide for their wives, parents have neglected their children, and grown sons and daughters have forsaken their elderly parents. Such neglect is solemnly condemned.

"If any one does not provide for his own, and especially for those of his household, he has denied the faith, and is worse than an unbeliever" (1 Timothy 5:8). Meeting the needs of your family and relatives is the first priority in giving and one in which there should be no compromise.

The Local Church, Christian Workers and Ministries

Throughout its pages the Bible focuses on supporting the Lord's ministry. The Old Testament priesthood was to receive specific support (Numbers 18:21), and the New Testament teaching on ministry support is just as strong. "Pastors who do their work well should be paid well and should be highly appreciated, especially those who work hard at both preaching and teaching" (1 Timothy 5:17, LB). How many Christian workers have been distracted from their ministry by inadequate support? Far too many.

People have asked Bev and me if we give only through our local church. In our case, the answer is no. However, we do give a minimum of 10 percent of our regular income through our church because we believe this is a tangible expression of our commitment to our church. But we also give to others who are directly having an influence on us. "And let the one who is taught the word share all good things with him who teaches" (Galatians 6:6).

The Poor

I didn't go to bed hungry last night, but conservative estimates are that one billion people in the world go to bed hungry each night. That is overwhelming. The number is so great that it may leave us feeling hopeless about what we can do. But Scripture consistently emphasizes our responsibility to give to the poor and the destitute.

In Matthew 25:34-45 we are confronted with one of the most exciting yet sobering truths in the Bible. Read this passage carefully:

> Then the King will say . . . "For I was hungry, and you gave Me something to eat; I was thirsty, and you gave Me drink . . ." Then the righteous will answer Him, saying, "Lord, when did we see You hungry, and feed You, or thirsty, and give You drink?" . . . The King will answer and say to them,

"Truly I say to you, to the extent that you did it to one of these brothers of Mine, even the least of them, you did it to Me." Then He will also say to those on His left, "Depart from Me, accursed ones, into the eternal fire . . . for I was hungry, and you gave Me nothing to eat; I was thirsty, and you gave Me nothing to drink . . . to the extent that you did not do it to one of the least of these, you did not do it to Me."

In some mysterious way that we cannot fully comprehend, Jesus personally identifies with the poor. Do you want to minister to Christ? You do so when you give to the poor. If that truth is staggering, then the reciprocal is terrifying. When we do not give to the poor, we leave Christ Himself hungry and thirsty.

Three areas of our Christian life are affected by our giving or our lack of giving to the poor:

1. Prayer
A lack of giving to the poor could be the cause of unanswered prayer. "Is this not the fast which I chose . . . divide your bread with the hungry, and bring the homeless poor into the house . . . then you will call, and the Lord will answer" (Isaiah 58:6-9). And, "He who shuts his ear to the cry of the poor will also cry himself and not be answered" (Proverbs 21:13).

2. Provision
Our provision is conditioned upon our giving to the needy. "He who gives to the poor will never want, but he who shuts his eyes will have many curses" (Proverbs 28:27).

3. Knowing Jesus Christ Intimately
One who does not give to the poor does not know the Lord intimately. "'He pled the cause of the afflicted and needy; then it was well. Is not that what it means to know Me?' declares the Lord" (Jeremiah 22:16).

Giving to the poor has been discouraged, in part, because of the government's failure with welfare programs. However, I want to challenge you to consider asking the Lord to bring one poor person into your life. This will be a significant step in your maturing in your relationship with Christ. I pray that you and I might be able to echo Job's statement: "I delivered the poor who cried for help, and the orphan who had no helper . . . I made the widow's heart sing for joy . . . I was eyes to the blind, and feet to the lame. I was a father to the needy, and I investigated the case which I did not know" (Job 29:12-16).

Although this area of giving can be frustrating at times, the potential benefits to the giver make it one of the most exciting and fulfilling areas in our entire Christian life.

CONTRAST

Society says: It is more blessed to receive than to give.

Scripture says: "It is more blessed to give than to receive" (Acts 20:35).

COMMITMENT

Establish a time each week when you can discuss and pray about giving. Use the time to review this chapter.

WORK—
WHO IS YOUR REAL BOSS?

AT AGE 29 ALLEN HITCHCOCK felt trapped. For six years he had worked as a clerk in a large department store.

He was competent, and the job paid moderately well. He longed, however, for a future in management, and as he looked around, he saw that all those who were promoted to management positions had college educations. So, by taking night courses, he completed his college requirements and earned a degree in business administration. The company soon promoted Allen to a job at a much higher salary.

> Sloth, like rust, consumes faster than labor wears.
> BENJAMIN FRANKLIN

The first few years were just as he had imagined—reasonable hours, good wages and attractive fringe benefits. Then the unexpected happened. The company expanded to Florida, and the Hitchcocks were transferred. The expansion schedule called for strict deadlines, and Allen assumed major responsibilities as an assistant manager. At first he enjoyed the excitement of the challenge; however, his five-day week soon became six, and his normal eight-hour day grew to 14 hours. On top of that, his new boss was so demanding that Allen began to experience a great deal of tension at work.

He now had more work and more responsibility, but as an assistant manager he no longer could earn overtime. As a result he made the same pay as he would have before the promotion, and resentment toward his employer was building. Allen began to wonder if management was worth the stress.

Allen's job frustrations are not unusual. Few people are completely satisfied with their jobs. Boredom, lack of fulfillment, fear of losing a job, inadequate wages, overwork and countless other pressures contribute to a high level of discontentment. Doctors, homemakers, secretaries, salespeople, blue-collar workers and managers—regardless of the profession, the frustrations are similar.

During a 50-year career the average person spends 100,000 hours working. Most of an adult's life is involved in work. Unfortunately, many just endure their work while ignoring the fact that 25 percent of their lives is devoted to a distasteful job. On the other hand, some people like work too much and neglect the other priorities of life.

People usually lean to one of two extremes: they either work as little as possible because work is unpleasant, or they tend to work all the time because it becomes overwhelmingly important. Scripture affirms the value of work but teaches that we should have a balance in work. Work is designed to develop our character. While enabling us to provide for our material well-being, work is a pathway to experiencing a more intimate relationship with the Lord and with other people. In order to find satisfaction and balance in our work, we need to understand what Scripture teaches about it.

BIBLICAL PERSPECTIVE OF WORK

Even before the Fall, when sin entered the human race, God instituted work. "The Lord God took the man and put him into the garden of Eden to cultivate it and keep it" (Genesis 2:15). The very first thing the Lord did with Adam was to assign him work. Despite what many have come to think, work was initiated for our benefit in the sinless environment of the Garden of Eden. After the Fall, work was made more difficult. "Cursed is the ground because of you; in toil you shall eat of it all the days of your life. Both thorns and thistles it shall grow for you; and you shall eat the plants of the field; by the sweat of your face you shall eat bread" (Genesis 3:17-19).

Work is so important that in Exodus 34:21 God gives this command: "You shall work six days, but on the seventh day you shall rest." The Old Testament believer was required to work six days. In the New Testament Paul is just as direct when he says, "If anyone will not work, neither let him eat" (2 Thessalonians 3:10). Examine the verse carefully. It says, "If anyone *will not* work . . ." It did not say, "If anyone *cannot* work. . . ." This principle does not apply to those who are mentally or physically unable to work. It is for those who are able but choose not to work.

> *Diligence is the mother of good fortune.*
> CERVANTES

A primary purpose of work is to develop character. While the carpenter is building a house, the house is also building the carpenter. Skill, diligence, manual dexterity and judgment are refined. A job is not merely a task designed to earn money; it is also intended to produce godly character in the life of the worker.

A close friend has a sister who has been supported by her parents for more than 30 years. She has never had to face the responsibilities and hardships involved with a job. As a consequence, her character has not been properly developed and she is immature in many areas of her life.

Honorable Professions
Scripture does not elevate any honest profession above another. There is dignity in all types of work, and a wide variety of vocations are represented in the Bible.

David was a shepherd and a king. Luke was a doctor. Lydia was a retailer who sold purple fabric. Daniel was a government worker. Paul was a tentmaker. Amos was a fig-picker. If God can use a fig-picker, He can certainly use us in our jobs. In fact, the Savior of the world was a carpenter. In God's economy there is equal dignity in the labor of an automobile mechanic and a president of General Motors, in the labor of a senior pastor and a secretary serving the church.

God's Part in Work

Scripture reveals three specific responsibilities the Lord has in connection with work.

1. God gives job skills.

Exodus 36:1-2 illustrates this truth: "And every skillful person in whom the Lord has put skill and understanding to know how to perform all the work." God has given each of us unique skills. People have widely varied abilities, manual skills and intellectual capacities. It is not a matter of one person being better than another; it is simply a matter of having received different capabilities.

2. God gives success.

The life of Joseph is a perfect example. "The Lord was with Joseph, so he became a successful man . . . his master saw that the Lord was with him and how the Lord caused all that he did to prosper in his hand" (Genesis 39:2-3). As we have seen, you and I have certain responsibilities, but we need to recognize that it is ultimately God who gives success.

3. God controls promotion.

Psalm 75:6-7 reads, "For promotion and power come from nowhere on earth, but only from God" (LB). As much as it may surprise you, your boss is not the one who controls whether or not you will be promoted. When you understand this, you will work with a different attitude. It should have a tremendous impact on the way you perform as an employee.

This perspective of God's part in work is a remarkable contrast to the way most people think. Most leave God out of work and believe that they alone control their success and promotions. However, those with a biblical understanding will approach work with an entirely different frame of reference. They can avoid one of the major reasons people experience stress and frustration in their jobs because they understand God's part in work.

Stop reading for a few minutes and think about that. God gives you your skills and controls your success and promotion. Think about how this change in perspective will influence you and your job.

OUR PART IN WORK

All of us have certain responsibilities related to our work. Scripture reveals we are actually serving the Lord in our work and not people. "Whatever you do, do your work heartily, as for the Lord rather than for men; knowing that from the Lord you will receive the reward of the inheritance. It is the Lord Christ whom you serve" (Colossians 3:23-24). This perspective has profound implications. Consider your attitude toward work. If you could see the person of Jesus Christ as your boss, would you try to be more faithful in your job? The most important question you need to answer every day as you begin your work is: For whom do I work? You work for Christ.

Whatever you do, do your work heartily, as for the Lord rather than for men.
COLOSSIANS 3:23

Work hard.
"Whatever your hand finds to do, verily, do it with all your might" (Ecclesiastes 9:10). "The precious possession of a man is diligence" (Proverbs 12:27). In Scripture hard work and diligence are encouraged while laziness is repeatedly condemned: "He also who is slack in his work is brother to him who destroys" (Proverbs 18:9).

Paul's life was an example of hard work. "With labor and hardship we kept working night and day so that we might not be a burden to any of you . . . in order to offer ourselves as a model for you, that you might follow our example" (2 Thessalonians 3:8-9). Your work should be at such a level that people will never equate laziness and mediocrity with God.

But do not overwork! Working *too* hard has reached epidemic proportions. A frantic, breathless, overcommitment to work pervades our culture. Hard work must be balanced with the other priorities of life. Clearly our first priority is our relationship with the Lord. "But seek first His kingdom and His righteousness" (Matthew 6:33). The second priority is the family.

If your job demands so much of your time and energy that you neglect your relationship with Christ or your family, then you are working too hard; perhaps the job is too demanding or your work habits need changing. If you tend to be a "workaholic," take extra precautions to guard against forsaking your other priorities.

Exodus 34:21 reads, "You shall work six days, but on the seventh day you shall rest; even during plowing time and harvest you shall rest." I believe this Old Testament principle of resting one day out of seven has application for us today. This has been difficult for me, particularly when I am working under the pressure of a project deadline or financial pressure.

Rest can become an issue of faith. Is the Lord able to make our six days of work more productive than seven days? Yes! The Lord instituted this weekly rest for our physical, mental and spiritual health. The diagram below illustrates the balance God wants in our lives.

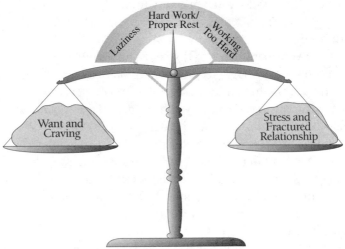

A Balanced Life with Contentment

EMPLOYER'S RESPONSIBILITIES

The godly employer must perform a balancing act. The employer is to love, serve and encourage the employee, but he or she must also provide leadership and hold employees accountable for their assigned tasks. Let's examine several principles that should govern an employer's conduct.

Serve your employees.

The basis for biblical leadership is servanthood: "Whoever wishes to become great among you shall be your servant" (Matthew 20:26). Too often employers have concentrated on producing a profit at the expense of their personnel. However, the Bible directs the employer to balance profit-making efforts with an unselfish concern for the employees. Employees are to be treated fairly and with genuine dignity. "Masters [employers], grant to your slaves [employees] justice and fairness, knowing that you too have a Master in heaven" (Colossians 4:1).

Employers should seek creative ways to serve their subordinates. For example, they should consider investing time and money to educate and upgrade their employees' job skills. As employees become more capable, both employees and companies can earn more.

Be a good communicator.

The biblical account of building the Tower of Babel teaches the importance of good communication. At that time everyone spoke the same language and adopted a common goal of building the tower. The Lord makes this remarkable observation, "If as one people speaking the same language they have begun to do this, then nothing they plan to do will be impossible for them" (Genesis 11:6, NIV).

Since building the tower was not what the Lord wanted, He stopped construction. And how did the Lord do this? He disrupted their ability to communicate. "Come, let us go down and confuse their language so they will not understand each other" (Genesis 11:7, NIV).

It is especially important to listen to employee complaints. "If I have despised the claim of my [employees] when they filed a complaint against me, what then could I do when God arises, and when He calls me to account, what will I answer Him?" (Job 31:13-14). A sensitive, listening ear is a tangible expression that you care about the other person. When a complaint is legitimate, the employer should take appropriate steps to solve the problem.

Hold employees accountable.

The employer is responsible for letting employees know what is expected of them on the job. The employer should regularly evaluate their performances and communicate this to them. If an employee is not performing satisfactorily and is unable or unwilling to change, a personnel change may be necessary.

Pay your employees a fair wage promptly.

Employers are warned to pay a fair wage. "[The Lord will judge] those who oppress the wage earner in his wages" (Malachi 3:5). They are also commanded to pay wages promptly when due. "You shall not oppress a hired [employee] . . . give him his wages on his day before the sun sets . . . so that he may not cry against you to the Lord and it become sin in you" (Deuteronomy 24:14-15).

EMPLOYEE'S RESPONSIBILITIES

We can identify the six major responsibilities of the godly employee by examining the well-known story of Daniel in the lions' den. In Daniel chapter 6 we are told that Darius, the king of Babylon, appointed 120 men to administer the government and three men, one of whom was Daniel, to supervise these administrators. When King Darius decided to promote Daniel to the job of governing the entire kingdom, Daniel's fellow employees tried to eliminate him. They first looked for an opportunity to discredit him in his job. After this failed, they persuaded King Darius to make a foolish decree. For a period of 30 days everyone in the kingdom would be required to worship the king only or suffer the punishment of death in the lions' den. Daniel was thrown to the lions because he continued to worship the living God. The Lord then rescued this godly employee by sending His angel to shut the lions' mouths.

Let's examine the attributes of a godly employee as displayed by Daniel.

Honest

Daniel 6:4 tells us that Daniel's fellow employees could find no grounds for accusation against him in regard to his work. "No evidence of corruption" could be found in Daniel's work. He was absolutely honest. We studied the importance of honesty earlier in the book.

Faithful
In Daniel 6:4, Daniel is described as "faithful." The godly employee needs to establish the goal of being faithful and excellent in work. Then he or she needs to work hard to attain that goal.

Prayerful
The godly employee is a person of prayer. "Now when Daniel knew that the document was signed [commanding worship of the king alone] . . . he continued kneeling on his knees three times a day, praying and giving thanks before his God, as he had been doing previously" (Daniel 6:10).

Daniel governed the most powerful nation of his day. Few of us will ever be faced with the magnitude of his responsibilities and the time demands that must have been required. Yet this man knew the importance and priority of prayer. If you are not praying consistently, your work is suffering.

Honors Employer
"Daniel spoke to the king, 'O king, live forever!'" (Daniel 6:21). What a remarkable response! The king, his employer, had been deceived and was forced into sentencing Daniel to the lions' den. But Daniel's reaction was to honor his boss. Think how natural it would have been to say something like, "You creep! The God who sent His angel to shut the lions' mouths is going to punish you!" Instead, he honored his employer.

The godly employee always honors his superior. First Peter 2:18 reads, "Servants [employees], be submissive to your masters [employer] with all respect, not only to those who are good and gentle, but also to those who are unreasonable." One way to honor your employer is never to participate in gossip behind your employer's back—even if he or she is not an ideal person.

Honors Fellow Employees
People will play "office politics" and may attempt to secure a promotion over you. They might even have you terminated from your

job. Daniel's peers tried to murder him. Despite this, no evidence exists that Daniel did anything but honor his fellow employees. Never slander a fellow employee. "Do not slander a slave [employee] to his master [employer], lest he curse you and you be found guilty" (Proverbs 30:10).

The godly person should avoid office politics and manipulation to secure a promotion. Your superior *does not* control your promotion. The Lord Himself makes that determination. We can be content in our jobs by striving for faithfulness, honoring superiors, loving and encouraging our fellow employees. Christ will promote us if and when He chooses.

Verbalizes His or Her Faith

At the appropriate time Daniel spoke of his faith in God to those around him. "The king spoke and said to Daniel, 'Daniel, servant of the living God, has your God, whom you constantly serve, been able to deliver you from the lions?'" (Daniel 6:20).

King Darius would never have known about the living God if Daniel had not communicated his faith at appropriate moments during the normal conduct of his job. King Darius would not have been as powerfully influenced by Daniel's profession of faith in God if he had not observed how he did his work. Daniel fulfilled his responsibilities with honesty and faithfulness while honoring those around him. Because of this demonstration, coupled with Daniel's deliverance from the lions, Darius became a believer: "I make a decree that in all the dominion of my kingdom men are to fear and tremble before the God of Daniel; for He is the living God and enduring forever, and His kingdom is one which will not be destroyed, and His dominion will be forever" (Daniel 6:26).

Daniel influenced his employer, one of the most powerful people in the world, to believe in the only true God. You have that same opportunity in your own God-given sphere of work. Let me say this another way. A job well done earns you the right to tell others with whom you work about the reality of Christ. As we view our work from God's perspective, dissatisfaction will turn to contentment from a job well done, and drudgery will be replaced with excitement over the prospect of introducing others to the Savior.

RETIREMENT

The dictionary defines retirement as "withdrawal from an occupation or business, to give up or retreat from an active life." The goal of retirement is deeply ingrained in our culture. Many people retire at an arbitrary, predetermined age and cease all labor in the pursuit of a life filled with leisure.

Scripture gives no examples of people retiring. Only one direct reference to retirement is found in the Bible. It is in Numbers 8:24-26; the instruction there applied exclusively to the Levites who worked on the tabernacle. As long as one is physically and mentally capable, no scriptural basis exists for retiring and becoming unproductive. The concept of putting an older but able person "out to pasture" is unbiblical. Age is no obstacle to finishing the work the Lord has for you to accomplish. For example, Moses was 80 years old when he began his 40-year task of leading the children of Israel.

Scripture does indicate that the type and intensity of work may change as we grow older—shifting gears to a less demanding pace and to becoming an "elder at the gate." During this season of life we can actively employ the experience and wisdom gained over a lifetime. I believe this should be the most rewarding and productive time of life. God has invested years in grooming us, and often we have more discretionary time.

Forget retirement. Grasp the opportunity to help build God's kingdom!

CALLING

Each of us has a specific calling or purpose which the Lord intends for us to fulfill in our work. Ephesians 2:10 reads, "For we are His workmanship, created in Christ Jesus for good works, which God prepared beforehand, that we should walk in them." Study this passage carefully. "We are His workmanship." Each of us has been created uniquely and given special physical, emotional and mental characteristics and abilities. You probably have heard the expression, "After the Lord made you, He threw away the mold!" It's true. You are gifted uniquely. No one in all of history—past, present or future—is like you.

The passage continues, "created in Christ Jesus for good works, which God prepared beforehand that we should walk in them." The Lord created each of us for a particular job, and He endowed us with the necessary skills, aptitudes and desires to accomplish this work. This calling may be full-time Christian service or a secular job. Often people struggle to know whether God wants them to continue in business once they have committed their lives to Christ. Many feel they are not serving the Lord in a significant way if they remain in a secular job. Nothing could be further from the truth. The key is for each person to determine God's call on his or her life.

Past experiences prepare us for our calling.
God providentially allows us to experience circumstances to prepare us for our calling. You might find it difficult to believe that God was molding you through your family, your environment, your education, your work and your relationships, especially if these were not godly influences. Nonetheless, He was preparing you even in the difficult experiences. For example, the Lord might use a painful, unwanted divorce to give someone the empathy and desire to serve others in a similar situation.

Knowing our calling allows us to focus.
Most of us struggle with too many things to do and too little time in which to do them. The good can become the enemy of the best. Once you have a clear vision of God's call on your life, it becomes much easier to evaluate opportunities and say "no" to those that would distract you from what the Lord wants you to accomplish.

I have two close friends. One has only average ability, but because he has been singled-minded in his focus he has had an enormous impact. The other man is much more capable but has scattered his energies pursuing numerous projects with limited success. Knowing your calling helps you focus and become more productive.

Someone has said, "Work as unto the Lord . . . the pay's not always great, but the retirement benefits are out of this world!" This is true, and you will find an additional benefit—increased satisfaction of a job done to the best of your ability.

CONTRAST

Society says: Work as little as possible because labor is distasteful; or work as much as possible because your job is all-important.

Scripture says: Work as unto the Lord with excellence as your standard. Work hard, but do not overwork.

COMMITMENT

Prayerfully evaluate your attitudes toward work and your job performance in light of what Scripture teaches. To help you discover any areas that need changing, ask yourself these questions:

1. Would I work more conscientiously if Jesus were my boss?
2. Would I think more highly of a president of an oil company than a gas station attendant?
3. How is my relationship with my employer, employees and fellow-workers?
4. Am I trying to do too much?
5. Am I performing my job at a level of excellence?
6. Am I lazy? Do I work hard?

INVESTING–
STEADY PLODDING

ONE PROBLEM Allen and Jean wanted to discuss was their inability to save. "We've never been able to save consistently," Jean admitted dejectedly. "We realize this has been a mistake, and we've suffered for it. Every time the car broke down or something else went wrong, we ended up going further in debt because we didn't have savings to pay for these unexpected expenses. What should we do?"

> *Steady plodding brings prosperity; hasty speculation brings poverty.*
> PROVERBS 21:5, LB

Allen added, "And how can we begin to invest to help provide for future needs such as our children's education and our retirement?"

Unfortunately, like the Hitchcocks most people are not regular savers. According to one source, the average person in our nation is three weeks away from bankruptcy. He or she has little or no money saved, significant monthly credit obligations and a total dependence on next week's paycheck to keep the budget afloat.

SAVING—THE JOSEPH PRINCIPLE

The Bible tells us it's wise to save. "The wise man saves for the future, but the foolish man spends whatever he gets" (Proverbs 21:20, LB).

Because of their instinct for saving, ants are commended for their wisdom: "Four things on earth are small, yet they are extremely wise: ants are creatures of little strength, yet they store up their food in the summer" (Proverbs 30:24, NIV). They put aside and save from the summer's plenty to meet a future need. Saving is the opposite of being in debt. Saving is making *provision for* tomorrow, while debt is *presumption upon* tomorrow.

Another example is Joseph, who saved during the seven years of plenty to ensure that there would be enough food during seven years of famine. I call saving the "Joseph Principle." Saving means to forego an expenditure today so you will have something to spend in the future. Perhaps this is why most people never save; it requires a denial of something that you want today, and our culture is not a culture of denial. When we want something, we want it *now*.

How to Save

When you receive income, the first check you write should be a gift to the Lord and the second check to your savings. The Bible does not teach an amount or percentage to be saved. We recommend establishing a goal of saving at least 10 percent of your income. For many this is not possible initially, but begin the habit of saving— even if it is only a dollar a month.

To develop this habit you can use several different methods. For example, some commit income from tax refunds or bonuses to savings. Others set aside a certain percent of their regular income each month in a savings account. Still others use a compulsory savings plan that is available through most banks or an employee payroll plan. Here is a maxim for saving: If you save a portion of your income as soon as you receive it, you will save more.

There are two types of savings: long-term and short-term.

Long-Term Savings
Long-term savings are intended to fund long-term needs and goals such as retirement income and inheritances. Pensions and retirement accounts fall into this category. Except for extreme financial

emergencies, these savings should not be used for any purpose other than the needs for which they were established.

Short-Term Savings

Short-term savings should be readily accessible. They may include interest-bearing accounts, mutual funds and so forth. These are designed to be used for planned future spending—acquiring or replacing items such as appliances and cars and making major home repairs. Short-term savings should also be set aside for emergencies—an illness, loss of job, or other interruption of income. Financial experts recommend you

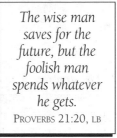

The wise man saves for the future, but the foolish man spends whatever he gets.
PROVERBS 21:20, LB

establish the goal of saving the equivalent of three to six months of your income for this emergency fund.

INVESTING

People place some of their savings in investments with the expectation of receiving income or a growth in value. The purpose and intention of this book is *not* to recommend any specific investments. Our objective is simply to draw your attention to the following scriptural framework for investing.

Be a Steady Plodder

"Steady plodding brings prosperity; hasty speculation brings poverty" (Proverbs 21:5, LB). The original Hebrew word for "steady plodding" pictures a person filling a large barrel, one handful at a time. Little by little the barrel is filled to overflowing.

The fundamental principle you need to practice to become a successful investor is to spend less than you earn. Then save and invest the difference over a long period of time.

Examine various investments. Almost all of them are well suited for "steady plodding." Your home mortgage is paid off after years of steady payments. A stock portfolio is built as it is added to each month, and a business can increase steadily in value through the years as its potential is developed.

Understand Compound Interest

The amazingly wealthy Baron Rothschild was once asked if he had seen the Seven Wonders of the World. He is reported to have responded, "No, but I do know the advantages of the eighth wonder of the world—compound interest." Understanding compounding is crucial. There are three variables in compounding: the amount you save, the interest rate you earn on your savings and the length of time you save.

1. *The amount.* The amount you save will be dictated by your level of income, the cost of your standard of living, how much debt you have and how faithfully you budget. It is our hope that you will be able to increase the amount available for saving as you implement the biblical principles.

2. *The interest rate.* The second variable is the rate of interest you earn on an investment. The following table demonstrates how an investment of $1,000 a year grows at various interest rates:

Interest	Year 5	Year 10	Year 20	Year 30	Year 40
6%	5,975	13,972	38,993	83,802	164,048
8%	6,336	15,645	49,423	122,346	279,781
10%	6,716	17,531	63,003	180,943	486,851
12%	7,115	19,655	80,699	270,293	859,142

As you can see, the increase in the rate of return has a remarkable impact on the amount accumulated. A two percent increase almost doubles the amount over 40 years. However, be wary of risky investments that promise a high return. Usually the higher the rate, the higher the risk.

3. *Time.* Time is a factor we cannot control, but the graph that follows may help you visualize the benefits of starting now. If a person faithfully saves $2.74 each day—$1,000 per year—and earns 10 percent on the savings, at the end of 40 years the savings will grow to $486,852 and will be earning $4,057 each month in interest alone! Steady plodding pays. However, if the person waits one year before starting, then saves for 39 years, he or she will accumulate $45,260 less. The moral of the illustration is this: Start saving now!

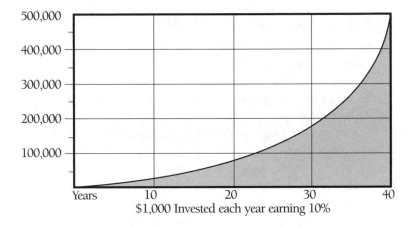

$1,000 Invested each year earning 10%

Avoid Risky Investments

> There is another serious problem I [Solomon] have seen everywhere—savings are put into risky investments that turn sour, and soon there is nothing left to pass on to one's son. The man who speculates is soon back to where he began— with nothing. This, as I said, is a very serious problem, for all his hard work has been for nothing; he has been working for the wind. It is all swept away (Ecclesiastes 5:13-16, LB).

Scripture warns of avoiding risky investments, yet each year thousands of people lose money in highly speculative and sometimes fraudulent investments. How many times have you heard of older people losing their life's savings on a get-rich-quick scheme? Sadly, it seems that Christians are particularly vulnerable to such schemes because they trust persons who seem to live by the same values they have. We have known of investment scandals in several local churches where wolves in sheep's clothing fleeced the flock. There are three characteristics often associated with risky investments:

- ◆ The prospect of a large profit is "practically guaranteed."
- ◆ The decision to invest must be made quickly. There will be no opportunity to thoroughly investigate the investment or the promoter who is selling the investment. The promoter will often be doing you a "favor" by allowing you to invest.
- ◆ Little will be said about the risks of losing money, and the investment will usually require no effort on your part.

Be patient when investing. I have never known anyone who made money in a hurry. Diligence, study and counsel are prerequisites for improving your chances for successful investments and for avoiding risky ones.

Diversify
"Divide your portion to seven, or even to eight, for you do not know what misfortune may occur on the earth" (Ecclesiastes 11:2). There is no investment without risk, and Scripture does not recommend any specific investments. Money can be lost on any investment. The government can make gold illegal. Real estate can suffer deflation or be taxed from you. Money can be inflated until it is valueless.

The perfect investment does not exist. We need to diversify. Consider the following steps as you diversify. I recommend that you not skip any of the steps. Start with step one, and take each step at a time.

Step 1: Save one month's living expenses and secure insurance protection.

Step 2: Save three to six months' living expenses; save for major purchases; develop your business and vocational skills.

A principle in Scripture is to invest in your business or vocation, which will be productive, then build your house: "Develop your business first before building your house" (Proverbs 24:27, LB). Many people today reverse this order. The large house, purchased too early in life, tends to require so much money that investing in business or vocation is seriously hampered.

Step 3: Purchase a home; invest conservatively to meet long-term goals.

Step 4: Make other investments.

George Fooshee talks about such investments in his excellent book, *You Can Be Financially Free.*

> Other investments are almost as varied as the imagination. Real estate, oil, stocks, bonds, antiques, coins, and virtually anything people collect can be considered investments. Some of these, such as stocks, bonds, and real estate, pay a return. Others are held with the expectation that they will increase in value as time goes by.
>
> Your investments beyond life insurance, vocation, and house should be matched with your own interests and personality. If you were raised on a farm and have knowledge of agricultural products and enjoy keeping abreast of the farm situation, then you might pursue a lifelong interest in agricultural investments. These could include everything from acquiring farmland to purchasing the stocks of those companies that are primarily agriculturally oriented.

Count the Cost

With every investment there are costs: financial costs, time commitments and efforts required. Sometimes investments can bring emotional stress. For example, the purchase of a rental house will require time and effort to lease and maintain. If the tenant is irresponsible, you may have to try to collect rent from someone who does not want to pay. Talk about emotions flaring! Before you decide on any investment, carefully consider all the costs.

Now we will shift our attention to a number of issues that are important to understand from God's perspective: balancing saving with giving, investment goals, gambling and leaving an inheritance.

GIVING, SAVING AND INVESTING

It is scripturally permissible to save and invest only when we are also giving. Jesus told a parable that illustrates the danger of saving while not giving.

The land of a certain rich man was very productive. And he began reasoning to himself, saying, "What shall I do, since I have no place to store my crops?" And he said, "This is what I will do: I will tear down my barns and build larger ones, and there I will store all my grain and my goods. And I will say to my soul, 'Soul, you have many goods laid up for many years to come; take your ease, eat, drink and be merry.'" But God said to him, "You fool! This very night your soul is required of you; and now who will own what you have prepared?" So is the man who lays up treasure for himself and is not rich toward God . . . For where your treasure is, there will your heart be also' (Luke 12:16-21, 34).

The key word in this parable is "all." Jesus called the rich man a fool because he saved *all* of his goods, laying them up for his own use. He did not balance his saving by giving generously. It is legitimate to save and invest only when we are also giving to the Lord. Why? "Where your treasure is, there will your heart be also" (Matthew 6:21).

If we concentrate solely on saving and investing, our focus and affection will gravitate there. We will be drawn inexorably to those possessions. But if we balance our saving and investing by giving generously to the Lord, we can still love Christ first with all our heart.

INVESTMENT GOALS

Before you develop your individual investment strategy, you should establish investment goals. I believe there are three acceptable goals for investing:

Providing for Your Family
First Timothy 5:8 reads, "If any one does not provide for his own, and especially for those of his household, he has denied the faith, and is worse than an unbeliever." This principle extends to providing for your needs in old age and leaving an inheritance to your children.

Becoming Financially Free to Serve the Lord

One objective of saving is to diminish our dependence upon a salary to meet our needs. This affords us the freedom to volunteer more time to ministry should this be what the Lord wants for us. The more my savings produce, the less I am dependent upon income from my work. Some have saved enough to be free one day a week, and others are in a position to be full-time volunteers without the need to earn a salary.

Operate Your Business

I believe it is proper to save and invest to accumulate enough capital to operate a business without going into debt. The amount of capital may vary substantially, depending upon the personnel and inventory requirements of each business.

Establishing a Maximum Amount

When a sprinter breaks the tape at the finish line, he stops running. But many people continue accumulating more and more, even though they have achieved the acceptable savings goals. I believe that each of us should establish a maximum amount we are going to accumulate, and once we have "finished this race," we should give away the portion of our income that we were saving. This "finish line" on accumulation protects us against the dangers of hoarding.

UNACCEPTABLE INVESTMENT GOALS

According to 1 Timothy 6:9-11 one investment goal, the desire to become rich, is strictly prohibited. First Timothy 6:9 states, "But those who want to get rich fall into temptation and a snare and many foolish and harmful desires which plunge men into ruin and destruction." Study this carefully. Everyone who wants to get rich will "fall into temptation and a snare and many foolish and harmful desires which plunge men into ruin and destruction."

For most of my life I wanted to become rich—not just a little rich—filthy rich! So dealing with the biblical prohibition against this attitude has been painful for me. Sometimes even now I vacillate between wanting to get rich and wanting to be a faithful steward. When I want to get rich, I am self-centered. My motivations for wanting to get rich may vary—pride, greed or an unhealthy compulsion to prepare for survival in an uncertain economic future. However, when I focus on being a faithful steward, I am Christ-centered in my thoughts and attitudes. My actions are then motivated by a pure heart. I am serving Christ and growing closer to Him.

The prohibition against wanting to get rich in 1 Timothy 6:9 is followed by this passage: "For the love of money is a root of all sorts of evil" (1 Timothy 6:10). In other words, when we want to get rich, Scripture tells us that we are loving money.

Matthew 6:24 says: "No one can serve two masters; for either he will hate the one and love the other, or he will hold to one and despise the other. You cannot serve God and mammon [money]." Think about this carefully. When we want to get rich, we are actually loving money and hating God. We are holding on to money and despising God. We are serving money, and we are therefore not serving the living God. First Timothy 6:10 ends by saying, "Some by longing for [riches] have wandered away from the faith, and pierced themselves with many a pang."

I have witnessed firsthand the truth of this Scripture. I deeply admired the man who led me to Christ, but he became consumed by a desire to get rich. He divorced his wife and abandoned his four young sons. Ultimately, he denied Christ and wandered away from the faith. Wanting to get rich, which is the love of money, is a devastating spiritual condition in which to be.

Understand me clearly. I am *not* saying getting rich is wrong. In fact, I rejoice to see God sovereignly enable a man or woman to prosper. Nothing is wrong with becoming wealthy if it is a by-product of being a faithful steward.

Split and Submit

We overcome the temptation to get rich by remembering to split and submit. In 1 Timothy 6:11 Paul counsels Timothy to "flee from these things [the desire to get rich], you man of God; and pursue righteousness, godliness, faith, love, perseverance and gentleness." When you become aware of your desire to become rich, you must flee (split) from that temptation and replace it with the pursuit of godliness.

Next, submit. The ultimate way of escape is found in submitting to Jesus as Lord. We can do this in perfect confidence because Jesus overcame a massive temptation to become rich. After Christ fasted 40 days in the wilderness, the devil tempted Him three times. The final temptation is recorded in Luke 4:5-7: "[The devil] led Him [Jesus] up and showed Him all the kingdoms of the world in a moment of time. And the devil said to Him, 'I will give You all this domain and its glory . . . if You worship before me.'" Can you imagine what an incredible temptation this would present?

When I was in the real estate development business and discovered a prime piece of property, I would almost immediately begin to covet it and revel in the possibility of becoming rich. Jesus was exposed to all the kingdoms of the world in a moment of time. But because He was submitted entirely to the Father and empowered by the same Holy Spirit who lives in us, He was able to resist that temptation.

I believe that our heavenly Father will never ultimately prosper His children when they are motivated to get rich. Wanting to get rich—loving money—closely parallels greed. And "greed . . . amounts to idolatry" (Colossians 3:5). The Father watches jealously over His children to ensure that we will not be drawn away from loving Him with all our hearts.

GAMBLING AND LOTTERIES

Government-sanctioned lotteries and all types of gambling are sweeping our nation. A recent study reported that the average church member gives $20 a year to foreign missions while the average person gambles $1,174 a year! Sadly, there are hundreds of thousands of compulsive gamblers who regularly deplete their family income. Their stories are heart-breaking. The Bible does not specifically prohibit gambling; however, many who gamble do so in an attempt to get rich quickly. This is a violation of Scripture.

As men and women who serve a holy God, we are called to be salt and light to a lost world. I firmly believe we need to make a commitment *never* to participate in gambling or lotteries even for entertainment. We should not expose ourselves to the risk of becoming compulsive gamblers, nor should we support an industry that enslaves so many.

INHERITANCE

Parents should attempt to leave a material inheritance to their children. "A good man leaves an inheritance to his children's children" (Proverbs 13:22). The inheritance should not be dispensed until the child has been thoroughly trained to be a wise steward. "An inheritance gained hurriedly at the beginning, will not be blessed in the end" (Proverbs 20:21).

In my opinion, you should provide for the inheritance to be distributed over several years or when the heir is mature enough to handle the responsibility of money. Select those you trust to supervise the youth until he or she is a capable steward. "Now I say, as long as the heir is a child, he does not differ at all from a slave although he is owner of everything, but he is under guardians and managers until the date set by the father" (Galatians 4:1-2).

You should provide an inheritance for your children. However, it probably is not wise to leave your children with great wealth if they have not been thoroughly schooled in the biblical perspective of money and how to properly manage it. Andrew Carnegie once said, "The almighty dollar bequeathed to a child is an almighty curse. No one has the right to handicap his children with such a burden as great wealth. He must face this question squarely: Will the fortune be safe with my child, and will my child be safe with my fortune?"

Wills

The majority of people who die do not have a current will. Think of what this means. To die without a will is expensive and time-consuming and can be heartbreaking for your loved ones. It can literally destroy an estate left to provide for the family.

Scripture teaches that we brought nothing into the world and we will take nothing with us when we die, but we *can* leave it behind precisely as we wish. We can specify to whom and how much. If you die without a will, these decisions are left up to the court. Under some circumstances the court can appoint a guardian (who may not know the Lord) to raise your children if you have not made this provision in your will.

Whether you are married or single, rich or poor, you should have a will. Not only does it clear up any legal uncertainties, it also helps you map out your finances while you are alive so that you can protect the best interests of your heirs.

About 36 out of 100 people die before retirement age. So do not put off preparation of your will just because you may be young. Do it now! As Isaiah told Hezekiah, "Thus says the Lord, 'Set your house in order, for you shall die'" (2 Kings 20:1). Someday, should the Lord tarry, you will die. One of the greatest gifts you can leave your family for that emotional time will be an organized estate and a properly prepared will or revocable living trust. If you do not have a current will or trust, please make an appointment with an attorney to prepare one.

CONTRAST

Society says: Spend all you make. However, if you should save, put your trust in your accumulated assets.

Scripture says: "The wise man saves for the future, but the foolish man spends whatever he gets" (Proverbs 21:20, LB).

COMMITMENT

1. Establish a pattern of saving. Start with your next paycheck.

2. Make an appointment with an attorney this week to have your will drawn.

TWELVE

THE ONE GUARANTEED INVESTMENT

I WAS 28 YEARS OLD when I stumbled upon the only fully guaranteed investment that exists. I started attending a weekly breakfast with several young businessmen and was impressed because they were astute and energetic. But more than that, I was attracted to the quality of their lives.

At the time I was part owner of a successful restaurant. I was married to my wonderful wife, Bev, and lived in a comfortable home. I had everything I thought would give me happiness and a sense of accomplishment, but I had neither. Something was missing. I was surprised to hear these men speak openly of their faith in God. I had attended church regularly when I was growing up. However, I never heard that it was possible to have a personal relationship with Jesus Christ.

A friend described how I could enter into this relationship with the Lord. He shared several biblical truths that I previously had not understood.

God loves you and wants you to know Him.

God created people in His own image, and He desires an intimate relationship with each of us. My friend directed my attention to two passages: "God so loved the world, that He gave His only begotten Son, that whoever believes in Him should not perish, but have eternal life" (John 3:16). "I [Jesus] came that they might have life, and might have it abundantly" (John 10:10).

When my son, Matthew, was in the first grade, he developed a burning desire to win the 100-yard dash at his school's field day. That was all we heard about for two months. But there was a problem: his classmate Bobby Dike was faster than Matthew.

Field day finally arrived. They ran the 50-yard dash first, and Bobby easily beat Matthew. I will never forget when Matthew came up to me with tears in his eyes, pleading, "Daddy, please pray for me in the 100-yard dash. I've just got to win." My heart sank as I nodded.

With the sound of the gun, Matthew got off to a quick start. Halfway through the race he pulled away from the rest of his classmates and won. I lost control of myself! I was jumping and shouting. I had never before experienced such exhilaration. Then it occurred to me how much I loved my son. Although I love other people, I do not love them enough to give my son to die for them. But that is how much God the Father loved you. He gave His only Son, Jesus Christ, to die for you.

We are separated from God.
God is holy. This means God is perfect, and He will not have a relationship with anyone who also is not perfect. My friend asked me if I had ever sinned—done anything that would disqualify me from being perfect. "Many times," I admitted. He explained that every person has sinned, and the consequence of sin is separation from God.

"For all have sinned and fall short of the glory of God" (Romans 3:23). "Your sins have cut you off from God" (Isaiah 59:2, LB).

This diagram illustrates our separation from God:

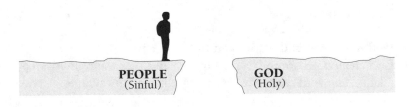

PEOPLE
(Sinful)

GOD
(Holy)

An enormous gap separates us from God. Individuals try without success to bridge this gap through their own efforts, such as living a good, moral life.

God's only provision to bridge this gap is Jesus Christ.
Jesus Christ died on the cross to pay the penalty for our sin and bridge the gap between us and God. "Jesus said . . . 'I am the way, and the truth, and the life; no one comes to the Father, but through Me'" (John 14:6). "But God demonstrates His own love toward us, in that while we were yet sinners, Christ died for us" (Romans 5:8).

This diagram illustrates our union with God through Jesus Christ:

PEOPLE
(Sinful)

GOD
(Holy)

This relationship is a gift from God.
My friend explained that by an act of faith I could receive the free gift of a relationship with God. The transaction appeared too good to be true. I had learned in business that anytime you had two people who were convinced they were getting more than they were giving up, you had a transaction. But now I was being offered a relationship with God, and it was a free gift. "For by grace you have been saved through faith; and that not of yourselves, it is the gift of God; not as a result of works, that no one should boast" (Ephesians 2:8-9).

We must each receive Jesus Christ individually.
I had only to turn away from (repent of) my sins and ask Jesus Christ to come into my life and become my Savior and Lord. And I did it.

As my business associates can tell you, I am a very practical person. They know that, if something does not work, I quickly stop it. Now, after 25 years' experience, I can confirm beyond a shadow of a doubt that a relationship with God can be yours through Jesus

Christ. Nothing I know of compares with the privilege of knowing Christ personally.

If you desire to know the Lord and are not certain whether you have this relationship, I encourage you to ask Christ to come into your life and settle this issue by repeating a simple prayer. "Father God, I need You. I invite Jesus to come into my life and make me the person You want me to be. Thank You for forgiving my sins and giving me the gift of eternal life."

You might fulfill each of the principles in becoming a faithful steward, but without a relationship with Christ, your efforts will be in vain. If you asked Christ into your life, begin to attend a church that teaches the Bible so that you can mature in your faith. Please contact Crown Ministries if we can answer any questions or help you in any way.

CHILDREN—
THE ABC'S OF MONEY

LEARNING TO HANDLE MONEY one step at a time is part of a child's education, a part that parents cannot leave to teachers but must direct themselves. Spending experiences are found in the outside world rather than in the classroom.

Bev and I met the Hitchcock family at the park for a picnic. As we watched their children play, Jean expressed a concern: "Allen and I were not trained by our parents to handle money responsibly, and I'm afraid we're not doing a much better job. Our children just don't understand the value of money. What should we do?"

This is a question all parents need to answer.

In 1904 the country of Wales experienced a remarkable revival. Thousands of people were introduced to Christ, and the results were dramatic. Bars closed because of a lack of business. Policemen exchanged their weapons for white gloves as crime disappeared. Horses did not understand their drivers because profanities were no longer uttered. Wales sent missionaries all over the world.

> *Train up a child in the way he should go, even when he is old he will not depart from it.*
> PROVERBS 22:6

One of those missionaries traveled to Argentina, where on the streets, he led a young boy to Christ. The boy's name was Luis Palau. He has since become known as the "Billy Graham" of Latin America. Out of gratitude for this Welsh missionary, Palau traveled to Wales during the early 1970s to express his thankfulness to that nation for helping lead him to Christ. What he discovered was astonishing. Less than one half of one percent of the Welsh attended church. Divorce was at an all-time high, and the crime rate was escalating rapidly. Many churches had closed and been converted to bars, and rugby had replaced Christianity as the national religion.

As a result of this experience, Palau produced a film entitled *God Has No Grandchildren*. The thrust of the film is that each generation is responsible for passing on the faith to the next. In Wales, despite tremendous spiritual vitality, the impact of Christianity had all but disappeared in 70 years. Parents had failed to pass their faith on to their children. Each generation is responsible for passing on to its children the gospel and the truths of Scripture, including God's financial principles.

Answer this question: When you left home, how well prepared were you to make financial decisions? Parents and teachers spend 18 to 22 years preparing youth for occupations but generally less than a few hours teaching children the value and use of the money they will earn during their careers.

To teach biblical principles of handling money, parents should use these three methods: verbal communication, modeling and practical experience.

Verbal Communication

The Lord charged the Israelites, "And these words, which I am commanding you today, shall be on your heart; and you shall teach them diligently to your sons and shall talk of them when you sit in your house and when you walk by the way and when you lie down and when you rise up" (Deuteronomy 6:6-7). We must verbally instruct our children in the ways of the Lord, but children need more than mere verbal instruction; they also need a good example.

Modeling

Children soak up parental attitudes toward money like a blotter soaks up ink. Parents need to be models of how to handle money faithfully. Paul recognized the importance of example when he said, "Be imitators of me, just as I also am of Christ" (1 Corinthians 11:1). The Lord used both of these techniques. He gave us His written Word, the Bible, and also sent the perfect model, Jesus Christ, to demonstrate how we should live.

Luke 6:40 is a challenging passage for parents. It reads, "Everyone, after he has been fully trained, will be like his teacher." Another way of saying this is that we can teach what we believe, but we only reproduce who we are. We must be good models.

Practical Experiences

Children then need to be given opportunities to apply what they have heard and seen. There are learning experiences which benefit the child in the area of money management (the art of wise spending) and money making (the value of work).

LEARNING EXPERIENCES IN "MONEY MANAGEMENT"

Learning to handle money should be part of a child's education. Parents must direct this themselves and not delegate it to teachers because spending experiences are found outside the classroom. Consider five areas where this is possible:

Income

As soon as the child is ready for school, he should begin to receive an income to manage. The parents need to decide whether they wish to give an allowance or require their child to earn the income. Choose the alternative with which you are most comfortable.

The amount of the income will vary according to such factors as the child's age and ability to earn. However, the amount is not as important as the responsibility of handling money. At first it is a new experience, and the child will make many mistakes. Don't hesitate to let the "law of natural consequences" run its course. You're going to be tempted to help little Johnny when he spends all his income the first day on an unwise purchase. You won't like the fact that he has to live the rest of the week without all the other things he wants and maybe needs. *Don't bail him out.* His mistakes will be his best teacher.

Parents should establish boundaries and offer advice on how to spend money, but your child must have freedom of choice. Excessive restrictions will only reduce his opportunities to learn by experience. The first few pennies and nickels will make a lasting impression. Every Saturday morning I used to bicycle to the store with my son Matthew to buy him a pack of his favorite gum. Despite my persistent advice, the entire pack would be consumed that first day.

When Matthew started to receive income, we decided that he would have to buy his own gum. I will never forget the pained look on his face as he came out of the store with his first purchase. "Daddy, this gum cost me all my money," he blurted. That pack was rationed with tender care and lasted more than a week.

Parents should slowly increase the income as the child grows in his ability and demonstrates wise spending patterns.

Budgeting

When children begin to receive an income, teach them how to budget. Begin with a simple system consisting of three boxes, each labeled by category—give, save and spend. The child distributes a portion of his income into each box. Thus, a simple budget is established using visual control. When the box is empty, there is no money to spend. Even a six-year-old can understand this method.

By the time a child is 12, he is old enough to be exposed to the family's budget. He will understand that he is growing up because he can now share in making plans for spending the family income. He will realize that each member has a responsibility for wise spending, regardless of who provides the income. As the child matures, he should participate in every aspect of the family budget. It will help him to realize the extent and limitations of the family income as well as how to make the money stretch to meet the family's needs.

At first the child may think that the family has so much money that it is impossible to spend it all. To help him visualize the budget, have the family income converted to a sack of dollars. Place these on a table and divide the "income" pile into the various "expense" piles representing the categories of spending. It is often difficult for children to grasp numbers because they are abstract. The dollars will provide a tangible way for a child to understand the family budget.

During the budget training, teach your child to become a wise consumer. Teach shopping skills, the ability to distinguish needs from wants and the fine art of waiting on the Lord to provide. Warn the child about the powerful influence of advertising and the danger of impulse spending.

When the child becomes a teenager, discontinue the allowance unless he presents a budget that accounts for how the last week's allowance was spent.

Giving

The best time to establish the personal habit of giving is when you are young. It is helpful for children to give a portion of their gifts to a tangible need they can visualize. For example, a child can understand the impact of his gift when his contribution is helping to construct the new church building or when it is buying food for a needy family he knows.

Dr. Richard Halverson, former chaplain of the U.S. Senate, gave his son Chris this rich heritage as a child. Through a ministry that serves poor children, Chris and his brother gave money to support a Korean orphan named Kim who had lost his sight and an arm during the Korean War. Chris was taught to feel that Kim was his adopted brother. One Christmas, Chris bought Kim a harmonica. It was Kim's first personal possession. He cherished this gift from Chris and learned to play it well. Today Kim is an evangelist, and in his presentation of the gospel he includes playing the harmonica. By being trained to give as a youth, Chris experienced firsthand the value of meeting people's needs and seeing God change lives as a result of faithful giving.

When your child is a teenager, a family or church mission trip to a Third World country can be a powerful experience. Direct exposure to abject poverty can initiate a lifetime of giving to the poor.

We also recommend a family time each week for dedicating that week's gifts to the Lord. It is important for the children to participate in this time of dedication and worship. The more involved children are with their parents in the proper handling of money, the better habits they will have as adults.

Saving and Investing

The habit of saving should be established as soon as the child receives an income. It is helpful to open a savings account for your child at this time. As the child matures, you also should expose him or her to various types of investments—stocks, bonds, real estate, etc.

Teach your children the benefits of compounding interest. If they grasp this concept and become faithful savers, they will enjoy financial stability as adults. Parents should demonstrate saving by doing so for something that will directly affect and benefit the children. A good example is a family vacation. Use a graph the children can fill in so they can chart the progress of the family's saving.

Children should have both short-term and long-term saving programs. The younger the child, the more important are short-term achievable goals. To a four-year-old, a week seems like a lifetime to save for a small purchase. He or she will not understand about saving for future education or retirement but will get excited about saving for a small toy. Long-term saving for education, the first car, etc. should be a requirement. Some parents find it motivating to their child if they match their child's contribution to their long-term savings.

Debt

It is also important to teach the cost of money and how difficult it is to get out of debt. Dick Getty loaned his son and daughter the money to buy bicycles. Dick drew up a credit agreement with a schedule for repayment of the loan. He included the interest charged. After they successfully went through the long, difficult process of paying off the loan, the family celebrated with a "mortgage burning" ceremony. Dick said that his children have appreciated those bikes more than any of their other possessions, and they have vowed to avoid debt in the future.

LEARNING EXPERIENCES IN "MONEY MAKING"

Because work is an essential element in becoming a faithful steward, parents have the responsibility to train each child in the value of work and proper work habits. If a child responds and learns how to work with a proper attitude, then he or she will not only have taken a giant step to becoming content, but he or she will become a valuable commodity in the job market. Good employees are difficult to find. Clearly, children need to learn the dignity and habit of work. There are four areas to consider in this training:

Establish routine responsibilities.
The best way for a child to become faithful in work is to establish the habit of daily household chores. For example, my daughter carries out the garbage and washes the dishes, and my son cleans the floors.

Expose your children to your work.
Not too many years ago most children were active participants in earning the family's money. They readily learned responsibility and the value of money. However, that is seldom the case today. Many children do not know how their father or mother earns the family income.

During a class several years ago, a participant said that he had asked his father what he did at work. "I make money," the father had responded. "For a long time I thought my dad actually made dollar bills. My mother would ask Dad, 'How much did you draw this week?' I thought he was a great artist to be able to do all that detailed lettering and artwork."

An important way to teach the value of work is to expose the child to the parents' means of earning a living. If your children cannot visit you at work, at least take the time to explain your job to them. For those parents who manage their own businesses, children should be encouraged to actively participate.

One word of advice, because most children no longer are with their parents at work, the parents' work attitudes and habits around the home will be a major modeling influence. If a parent works hard at the office but complains about washing the dishes at home, what's being communicated to the children about work? Examine your work attitudes and activities at home to ensure that you are properly influencing your children to be godly workers.

Earn extra money at home.
You should encourage your child to do extra work to earn money. A good rule of thumb is to pay the child a fair wage for the work you would have to hire someone to do. For example, if your car needs washing and your daughter needs some extra money and wants to wash it, let her. Be happy to pay her rather than the person at the car wash.

Encourage your child to work for others.
A paper route, baby-sitting job, janitorial work or waiting tables will serve as an education. A job gives a child an opportunity to enter into an employee-employer relationship and to earn extra money.

As your child enters high school it is a good idea to discontinue allowances during summer vacation. This will motivate him to earn his own money by holding a summer job. Moreover, some students can handle part-time work during the school year.

The objective of training your child in the value of work is to build and discipline his character. A working child with the proper attitude will be a more satisfied individual. He or she will grow up with more respect for the value of money and what is required to earn it.

Dependence, Danger and Destruction

Fathers in our country spend less time with their children than fathers in almost every other nation of the world. Fathers currently spend an average of only 37 seconds per day communicating with their sons. David and Eli were both godly men who had remarkably productive careers. Yet both lost sons through careless fathering.

If children are going to thrive, it will be because parents place them high on their list of priorities, consistently reserving an adequate portion of their time and energy for leadership within their homes. Fathers, I plead with you to seize the opportunity to train your children. You can literally influence generations.

It is very common these days for a single mother to be the head of the household. I appreciate the demands these mothers face. But please be encouraged. Some of the most responsible children I have ever met have been raised by godly mothers alone.

Dependence on Prayer

One of the most valuable lessons you can teach your children is to pray for the Lord's guidance and provision. The Lord wants to demonstrate that He is actively involved in each of our lives. One way He does this is by answering our prayers. Because of our affluent society, we often rob ourselves of this opportunity. We can buy things or charge purchases without prayerfully allowing the Lord to supply them. We need to be creative in how we can experience the reality of God in the area of our spending, and we need to be careful to communicate that value to our children.

Danger of Television

Television has affected children in ways we have not yet begun to fathom. Consider these statistics: by the time the typical teenager graduates from high school, he has spent 10,800 hours in class and 15,000 hours in front of the "tube." Children spend more time watching television (30 to 50 hours a week) than any other activity except sleeping. A recent survey asked children if they would rather give up television or their fathers. More than two out of five, 44 percent, responded they would forsake their fathers.

Most of the damage does not come from programs or commercials that directly attack biblical standards but from those that make anti-scriptural assumptions and whose attack is subtle and indirect. The influence of television on children is so pervasive and potentially dangerous that parents cannot afford to ignore it. Rather, they must restrict and regulate television if they are to be successful in training their children to be faithful stewards.

Destruction of Over Indulgence

When it comes to money, parents are always on a tightrope trying to keep a proper balance. They can easily be too miserly with money. In our affluent culture, however, they are more often over indulgent, and consequently hamper the development of their child's character.

How many of us know of a father who once sold newspapers to earn a bicycle and now has a teenage son who drives a sports car? Clearly, over indulgence with money can retard the development of a child's character and destroy the need for initiative and motivation. Too often it creates in a child a constant expectation to be given things without having to work or save for them.

Strategy for Independence

Finally, we need to establish a strategy for independence. Lyle and Marge Nelsen of Orlando have four of the most mature and responsible children I have ever met. Their strategy has been to work toward having each child independently managing all of his or her own finances (with the exception of food and shelter) by the senior year in high school. In this way they could be available to advise the children as they learn to make spending decisions.

Let's review the three steps for training children:

1. *Verbally communicate* biblical principles of handling money. Crown Ministries has developed a series of three studies for children—one for teens, one for children ages 8 to 12, and a study for children under 8. Parents can use these very effectively to train their children.

2. *Become models* of financial faithfulness, allowing your children to observe closely how you apply these principles.

3. *Create practical opportunities* for your children to experience God's financial principles. Each child has an individual personality and temperament. One child may spend wildly yet be very generous; another may save everything and never want to give. You need to study your children's personalities carefully and tailor the training to fit the child.

As the country of Wales discovered, God has no grandchildren. Passing on our faith in Christ to the next generation can be compared to a relay race. Any track coach will tell you that relay races are often won or lost in the passing of the baton from one runner to another. Seldom is the baton dropped once it is firmly in the grasp of a sprinting runner. If it is going to be dropped, it is in the exchange that takes place between the runners. As parents we have the responsibility to pass the baton of practical biblical truths to our children. At times during the training it may seem as if there is little progress. *Nonetheless, be consistent and persistent!*

I have yet to meet an adult whose parents lived all of these biblical financial principles and taught them systematically to their children. As an unfortunate consequence of this lack of training, children have left home ill-equipped to manage their financial future according to Scripture. I pray our generation will leave our children the blessed legacy of financial faithfulness.

CONTRAST

Society says: Parents need not require their children to establish the discipline of managing money or of working hard.

Scripture says: Parents have the obligation to train a child to be a faithful steward and a wise money manager.

COMMITMENT

Evaluate what your children are learning about work and handling money. Consider using the Crown Ministries children's studies to train them to become faithful stewards.

BUDGET—
KEEP ABREAST OF THE FACTS

THE DAY BEV AND I went to see Jean Hitchcock's parents, Frank and Vivian Webster, they were enjoying the visit of their youngest granddaughter, Heather. As they watched her play, there was not even a hint of what they had gone through the previous year. For the Websters it had been a year of dramatic upheaval. Frank had suffered a stroke that paralyzed his left side and caused him to lose his job. They were forced to sell their cozy lakefront home and readjust to a much lower standard of living.

The clean, neat apartment they now called home was sparsely furnished. It was apparent that they were going through hard times. Vivian explained their readjustment. "We have been amazed at what we can live without. We have been forced to watch every penny and follow a strict budget."

Annual income twenty pounds, Annual expenditure nineteen six, Result happiness.

Annual income twenty pounds, Annual expenditure twenty pounds ought and six, Result misery.
CHARLES DICKENS

Their backs were against a financial wall, and the Websters had responded by economizing at every turn. They went without air conditioning, no longer ate at restaurants and limited the use of the hot water heater to 30 minutes a day—just enough for showers and the dishes. Their conservation was paying off. They were actually putting more money into savings than when they were living on Frank's lucrative salary as an engineer. However, during those years of easy spending, they had lived without the restraints of a budget.

"The trauma of unemployment forced us to communicate in an area of our lives that had been 'off limits' during the 'good old days,'" Vivian explained. "We have learned more about each other through this adversity than at any other time during our 37 years of marriage. As strange as this may sound, we are grateful that this hardship happened. There is more peace in our family now than during the years of prosperity."

What Is a Budget?

The Websters are proof that when we plan where our money is to go, we can make the money go further. That's what a budget is—a plan for spending money.

Why Budget?

When the bank notified the depositor of his overdraft he replied in disbelief, "I must have more money left in my account. I still have six checks in my checkbook!" Like the surprised depositor, if you do not have a written budget, chances are that you are flying by the seat of your financial pants.

Budgeting is not always fun, but it is the only way to follow through and apply what has been learned about getting out of debt, saving and giving while still meeting basic needs. Regardless of income, most of us have difficulty making ends meet unless there is a plan for spending. Expenses always tend to rise just a little higher than income. I have seen countless examples of this. Regardless of what a person earns, he or she probably will have "too much month at the end of the money" unless a carefully planned and disciplined approach to spending is established and followed. Using a budget introduces an attitude of control in spending that is needed to reach financial objectives.

Budgeting provides an opportunity to pray about spending decisions.
This is important because according to a survey of young husbands, more than 50 percent of the most serious marital problems are financial. In fact, one judge has said, "Quarreling about money is the major reason for our unprecedented divorce rate." I seldom see a family with financial problems where there is not real tension within the marriage.

A successful budget should be a team effort. It is a good communication tool for the husband and wife to use. A budget also can help a family get full value for its money without losing sight of the things its members want most.

A family in our neighborhood is committed to sending their children to camp each summer for two weeks. Several years ago as they were planning their annual budget in January, it became apparent that there would not be enough money for the children to go to camp. The family then agreed each member would "contribute" to summer camp by making a sacrifice: The father gave up his golf game once a month, the mother did not join her summer bowling league and the children received half their normal allowance. By using a budget, the family was able to anticipate a problem and adjust their spending to enable them to get what they wanted most, in this case, summer camp.

How to Budget

A budget is useful only if it is used. It should be a plan tailor-made for managing *your* finances, not someone else's. Some people are more comfortable using a hand-written system, while others prefer using a budget system on computer.

To set up your budget follow these three steps:

Step One
Begin where we are today
Developing a budget must begin with the current situation. Determine precisely how much money is earned and spent. Most people do not know what they are actually earning and spending. For this

reason it is essential to keep a record of every penny for a month to get an accurate picture in order to complete an estimated budget.

If your wages are not the same each month (like the income of a commissioned salesperson), make a conservative estimate of your annual income and divide by 12 to establish a working figure for your monthly income.

Then determine which expenses do not occur each month. Examples are real estate taxes and vacations. Estimate how much you spend for these each year and divide that amount by 12 to determine your monthly cost. Armed with this information, you can complete accurately the Estimated Monthly Budget on the next page. Do not be discouraged. Almost every budget starts out with expenditures in excess of income. But a solution exists.

Step Two
The solution is where we want to be

To solve the problem of spending more than you earn, you must either increase your income or decrease your expenditures. It is that simple: Either earn more or spend less. There are no other alternatives.

Adding to Your Income

A part-time job, or better yet, a project that would involve the whole family are ways of increasing your income. The ever-present danger of increasing income is the tendency for expenses also to rise. To avoid this problem agree ahead of time to apply any extra income to balancing the budget. Another potential problem is that a family member may sacrifice relationships in order to earn extra money.

Reducing Expenses

My father was in the hotel business when I was growing up. He owned a small resort in Florida that catered to tourists. Business was seasonal; during the winter it flourished, but in the summer it withered to almost nothing. He tells me that just the thought of summer sent chills down his spine, but after the lean months he was always grateful. Summer taught him the habit of asking these questions about his expenses: Which are absolutely necessary?

ESTIMATED MONTHLY BUDGET

GROSS MONTHLY INCOME: _____

    Salary: _____

    Interest: _____

    Dividends: _____

    Other Income: _____

LESS:

  1. Giving: _____

  2. Taxes (Fed., State, FICA): _____

NET SPENDABLE INCOME: _____

LIVING EXPENSES: _____

  3. **Housing:** _____

    Mortgage or Rent: _____

    Insurance: _____

    Property Taxes: _____

    Electricity: _____

    Heating/Gas: _____

    Water: _____

    Garbage Service: _____

    Telephone: _____

    Mantainance: _____

    Cleaning & Supplies: _____

    Other: _____

  4. **Food:** _____

  5. **Transportation:** _____

    Payments: _____

    Gas & Oil: _____

    Insurance: _____

    Maint./Repair/Replace: _____

    Other: _____

  6. **Insurance:** _____

    Life: _____

    Medical: _____

    Other: _____

  7. **Debts:** _____

(except auto & house payments)

8. **Entertainment/Recreation:** _____

    Babysitters: _____

    Vacation: _____

    Pets: _____

    Other: _____

9. **Clothing:** _____

10. **Savings:** _____

11. **Medical Expenses:** _____

    Doctor: _____

    Prescriptions: _____

    Other: _____

13. **Miscellaneous:** _____

    Toiletries/Cosmetics: _____

    Laundry/Cleaning: _____

    Allowances: _____

    Subscriptions: _____

    Birthdays/Anniversaries: _____

    Weddings/Showers: _____

    Christmas Presents: _____

    Postage: _____

    Accounting/Legal: _____

    Education: _____

    Other: _____

13. **School/Child Care:** _____

    Tuition: _____

    Day Care: _____

    Other: _____

14. **Investments:** _____

TOTAL LIVING EXPENSES: _____

INCOME VS. LIVING EXPENSES:

Net Spendable Income: _____

Less Total Living Expenses: _____

Surplus or Deficit: _____

Which can I do without? Which can I reduce?

You can ask these same questions of your personal budget as you work to reduce spending.

Here are some guidelines to help you evaluate your major expenses. Actual percentages may vary depending upon the cost of housing where you live, the size of your family and your income. When you exceed the upper range in a category, this should warn you to carefully evaluate your spending in that category.

PERCENTAGE GUIDELINE	
Category	Percent of Income (after giving and taxes)
Housing	25-38%
Food	10-15%
Transportation	10-15%
Insurance	3-7%
Debts	0-10%
Entertainment / Recreation	4-7%
Clothing	4-6%
Savings	5-10%
Medical / Dental	4-8%
Miscellaneous	4-8%
School / Child Care	5-10%
Investments	0-15%

Consider these suggestions to spend more wisely:

Shelter

1. Purchase an older house that you can improve with your own labor. You can also buy a modest-size house suitable to your needs today with a design that can be expanded to meet your future needs.
2. Consider apartment living. It is less expensive and involves fewer responsibilities—lawn care, maintenance, etc.
3. If you can do repair and maintenance work such as lawn care, pest control, painting and carpet cleaning, you will save a substantial amount.

4. Lower the cost of utilities by limiting the use of heating, air conditioning, lights and appliances.
5. Shop carefully for furniture and appliances. Garage sales are a good source for reasonably priced household goods.

Food

1. Prepare a menu for the week. Then list the ingredients from the menu and shop according to the list. This will help you plan a nutritionally balanced diet, avoid impulse shopping and eliminate waste.
2. Shop once a week. Each time we go shopping for "some little thing," we always buy "some other little thing" as well.
3. Cut out the ready-to-eat food, which has expensive labor added to the price.
4. Leave children and hungry spouses at home when shopping. The fewer distractions from the list the better.
5. Lunches eaten out are often budget breakers. A lunch prepared at home and taken to work will help the budget and the waistline.
6. Reduce the use of paper products. Paper plates, cups and napkins are expensive to use.

Transportation

1. If it is possible to get by with one car, this will be the biggest transportation savings.
2. Purchase a low-cost used car and drive it until repairs become too expensive.
3. The smaller the car, the more economical to operate. You pay an estimated 35 cents a pound each year to operate an automobile.
4. Perform routine maintenance yourself—oil changes, lubrication, etc. Regular maintenance will prolong the life of your car.

Clothing

1. Make a written list of yearly clothing needs. Shop from the list during the off-season sales, at economical clothing stores and at garage sales.

2. Purchase simple basic fashions that stay in style longer than faddish clothes.
3. Do not purchase a lot of clothing. Select one or two basic colors for your wardrobe, and buy outfits that you can wear in combination with others.
4. Purchase home-washable fabrics. Clothes that must be commercially cleaned are expensive to maintain.

Insurance

1. Select insurance based on your *need* and budget, and secure estimates from three major insurance companies.
2. Raising the deductible feature will substantially reduce premiums.
3. Seek the recommendation of friends for a skilled insurance agent. A capable agent can save you money.

Health

1. Practice preventive medicine. Your body will stay healthier when you get the proper amount of sleep, exercise and nutrition.
2. Practice proper oral hygiene for healthy teeth and to reduce dental bills.
3. Ask friends to recommend reasonable and competent physicians and dentists.

Entertainment and Recreation

1. Plan your vacation for the off-season and select destinations near home.
2. Rather than expensive entertainment, seek creative alternatives such as picnics or exploring free state parks.

Five Budgeting Hints

1. Reconcile your checkbook each month.
2. It is helpful to have a separate savings account where you can deposit the monthly allotment for the bills that do not come due each month. For example, if your annual insurance premium is $960, deposit $80 in this savings

account each month. This ensures the money will be available when these payments come due.

3. We are trained to think monthly. To better understand the impact of an expense, figure the yearly cost. For example, if you spend $6 for lunch each working day, multiply $6 by five days a week by 50 weeks a year. It totals $1,500 for lunches. Thinking yearly shows the true cost of seemingly inconsequential expenses.

4. Control impulse-spending. Impulse-spending ranges from buying big things like automobiles to small items like tools. Each time you have the urge to spend for something not planned, post it to an "impulse list" and pray about the purchase for several days. As you do this, the impulse will often pass.

5. It is wise for husbands and wives to include personal allowances in the budget. Both should be given allowances to spend as they please. The wife can participate in her favorite hobby, and the husband can play golf as often as he likes, so long as the allowance holds out. This will eliminate many arguments.

Step Three
Do not stop!

The most common temptation is to stop budgeting. Don't do it. Frankly, many people find it difficult to begin a budget by themselves. If you have not yet enrolled in the Crown Ministries small group study, I challenge you to do so. In the small group environment you will be encouraged yet held accountable to implement biblical financial principles.

Remember, a budget is simply a plan for spending your money. It will not work by itself. Every area of your budget should be regularly reviewed to keep a rein on spending. "Any enterprise is built by wise planning, becomes strong through common sense, and profits wonderfully by keeping abreast of the facts" (Proverbs 24:3-4, LB).

Through the years there will be frustrations, but a budget, if properly used, will save you thousands of dollars. It will help you accumulate savings and will help you stay out of debt. More importantly, it will help husbands and wives communicate in an area that is a leading cause of marital conflict.

COMMITMENT

Keep a careful record of all expenditures for 30 days to determine your current situation. After that, plan a budget suited to your income and personal objectives. Put it into effect.

FIFTEEN

STANDARD OF LIVING—
HOW SHALL WE THEN LIVE?

I WAS INVITED TO ATTEND the second anniversary of a very special event, the day the Hitchcocks reached their goal of becoming debt-free. Two years later they were just as grateful for their new freedom and, more importantly, their marriage was growing stronger. Although it had been a struggle for them, and several times they had been on the verge of quitting, the stakes of saving their marriage were too high. They persevered and reached their goal.

> "Let temporal things serve your use, but the eternal be the object of your desire."
> THOMAS Á KEMPIS

Allen and Jean were now facing a new challenge, their income now exceeded their expenses. How should they spend the *surplus*? They had major decisions to make. Should they move to a larger home or stay in their present one and work on paying off the mortgage? Should they purchase a new car? Should they adopt a more expensive lifestyle or continue to save and give more?

The Bible does not dictate one particular standard of living for everyone. However, Scripture contains a number of challenging principles that we should consider when choosing our lifestyle.

Think with an eternal perspective.

Nurture an eternal perspective. Our culture and the media implore us to focus on the immediate. Advertisers persuade consumers to gratify themselves today with no thought of tomorrow. Examine the following to understand how brief life is on earth compared with eternity:

Our momentary time on earth is but a dot on the timeline of eternity. Yet, we have the opportunity to influence eternity by how we handle money today. We have not only the privilege to lay up treasures for ourselves in heaven but also the opportunity to spend money to influence people for Jesus Christ. Gaining eternal perspective and eternal values will have a profound effect on your decision making.

Moses is a good example. Study Hebrews 11:24-26 carefully: "By faith Moses, when he had grown up, refused to be called the son of Pharaoh's daughter; choosing rather to endure ill-treatment with the people of God, than to enjoy the passing pleasures of sin; considering the reproach of Christ greater riches than the treasures of Egypt; for he was looking to the reward."

Moses faced a choice. As Pharaoh's adopted son he could enjoy the lavish lifestyle of royalty, or he could choose to become a Hebrew slave. Because he had an eternal perspective, he chose the latter and was used by the Lord in a remarkable way. We face a similar decision. We can either live with a view toward eternity or live focused on this present world.

Have you ever returned as an adult to a place you knew as a child? I once visited a field on which I played when I was 12 years old. I remembered it as a huge field surrounded by towering fences. I was shocked to discover how small it really was! Or do you remember wanting to get something so much you could almost taste it? Yet, today it means almost nothing to you. I think we will experience something similar after we arrive in heaven. Many things that seem so important to us now will fade into insignificance in the light of eternity.

I encourage you to read *Money, Possessions and Eternity* by Randy Alcorn. It is a powerful and motivating study about living with an eternal perspective.

You are a pilgrim.

Scripture tells us about our identity and role on earth: First of all, we are citizens of heaven, not earth (Philippians 3:20). Second, we are ambassadors representing Christ on this earth (2 Corinthians 5:20). Third, we are aliens, strangers and pilgrims on this earth (Hebrews 11:13).

Peter wrote, "Since you call on a Father who judges each man's work impartially, live your lives as strangers here in reverent fear" (1 Peter 1:17, NIV). Later he added, "I urge you, as aliens and strangers in the world, to abstain from sinful desires, which war against your soul" (1 Peter 2:11, NIV).

The pilgrim is a traveler and not a settler—one who is acutely aware that the excessive accumulation of things can only distract from reaching the goal or destination. Material possessions are valuable to a pilgrim only as they facilitate his mission. The pilgrim is a traveler who chooses possessions strategically, regarding most of them as encumbrances that would slow the journey or make it impossible. Of course, many of us become "settlers" in the temporal sense, living in houses and owning furniture and developing businesses. There is nothing wrong with this, but we need to maintain a pilgrim mentality of detachment—the traveler's philosophy of traveling light.

Acquire only those possessions that enable you to fulfill God's calling on your life.

Make an effort to live simply.

Every possession requires time, attention and often money to maintain it. Too many or the wrong types of possessions can demand so much time, energy or money that they harm our relationship with the Lord and others. The quiet, simple life is the best environment to allow us enough time to nurture our relationship with the Lord. First Thessalonians 4:11-12 counsels, "Make it your ambition to lead a quiet life and attend to your own business and work with your hands, just as we commanded you; so that you may behave properly toward outsiders and not be in any need."

We are at war.

"Suffer hardship with me, as a good soldier of Christ Jesus. No soldier in active service entangles himself in the affairs of everyday life, so that he may please the one who enlisted him as a soldier" (2 Timothy 2:3-4). In wartime, people often alter their lifestyles radically to help win the war. They ration the use of strategically important items. They spend less on life's comforts so that the army will be adequately supplied. As soldiers, we should be careful not to become unduly encumbered with the cares of this life.

Recognize the enemy.

"For our struggle is not against flesh and blood, but against . . . the spiritual forces of wickedness in the heavenly places" (Ephesians 6:12). In a war you are going to use your most effective weapon. The devil's mission is to divert us from serving Christ. He frequently accomplishes this by tempting us to serve money and possessions. As we have seen before, money is the primary competitor with Christ for the lordship of our life. "You cannot serve God and mammon [money]" (Matthew 6:24).

Serving money is often difficult to identify because loving money is a respectable sin—people will congratulate you for acquiring the trappings of financial success. Therefore, you should prayerfully examine your relationship with Christ and money.

Spend in a way that pleases the Lord.

Prayerfully submit spending decisions to the Lord. Everything we possess is owned by the Lord, and we should spend to please Him and not for a selfish purpose. Seeking the Lord's direction in spending does not mean that we will never spend for anything other than a basic necessity. Recreation, appropriate leisure activities and rest are important. "For everything created by God is good, and nothing is to be rejected, if it is received with gratitude" (1 Timothy 4:4).

Do not waste possessions.

"There was a certain rich man who had a steward, and this steward was reported to him as squandering his possessions. And he called him and said to him, 'What is this I hear about you? Give an account of your stewardship, for you can no longer be a steward'"

(Luke 16:1-2). Examine yourself. Do you spend money frivolously or waste possessions habitually?

Do not compare yourself to others.

Some use comparison to justify spending more than they should. Many have suffered financially because they tried but could not afford to "keep up with the Joneses." Someone once said, "You can never keep up with the Joneses. Just about the time you catch them, they refinance their home and go deeper in debt to buy more things!" If you are wealthy, your lifestyle should be based on the conviction that the Lord wants you to have a certain standard of living which is not necessarily dictated by the maximum you can afford.

If only I had more. . . .

Have you ever felt that if only you were in a more prestigious position or had more money, then you could accomplish really significant things for the Lord?

Let's examine two men who lived in Rome and were at different ends of the economic spectrum. Before gladiator contests in the coliseum, everyone would stand, waiting silently for Caesar. The contests could not begin until he arrived. When Caesar arrived, he was greeted with thunderous shouts of "Hail Caesar!" He had more power, prestige and wealth than anyone else living at that time. He was worshipped as though he were a god.

Elsewhere in Rome was another man in vastly different circumstances. He was in prison, chained to guards. He invested his time praying and writing to his friends. His name was Paul.

One man lived in an opulent palace. The other lived in a dingy cell. One had almost unlimited wealth. The other had almost nothing. One was the center of attention. The other was virtually ignored. Almost 2,000 years later, people around the world recognize which of these two men made the eternally important contribution. They name their children after the prisoner and their salads after the emperor!

Being used by Christ in a significant way has nothing to do with a high position or great riches. It has everything to do with a willingness to allow Christ to become your Lord.

Do not be conformed to this world.

Romans 12:2 begins with this command, "Do not be conformed to this world." The Amplified Version reads this way: "Do not be conformed to this world—this age, fashioned after and adapted to its external, superficial customs."

We live in one of the most affluent cultures the world has ever known. And we are constantly bombarded with costly, manipulative advertising whose purpose is to prompt us to spend money. Advertisers usually stress the importance of image rather than function. For example, automobile ads rarely focus on a car as reliable transportation that is economical to operate; instead, an image of status or sex appeal is projected.

Reflect on the claims of TV commercials. No matter what the product—clothing, deodorants, credit cards, cars, beverages, you name it—the message is communicated that the "fulfilling, beautiful, wrinkle-free life" can be ours if we are willing to buy it. Unfortunately, this media onslaught has influenced all of us to some extent. George Fooshee, the author of the excellent book *You Can Beat the Money Squeeze*, so aptly states, "People buy things they do not need with money they do not have to impress people they do not even like."

The following graph depicts how the artificial, media-generated lifestyle influences our lives. The bottom curve represents our income—what we really can afford to buy. The next curve illustrates how much we actually spend. We make up the difference between our income and spending by the use of debt, which creates slavery, financial pressure and anxiety. The top of the graph demonstrates what advertisers tell us to buy. It is an image-conscious, generally expensive lifestyle that claims to satisfy the human heart's deepest needs. When we want to live this counterfeit, media-induced dream but cannot afford it, we suffer discontentment, envy and coveting.

None of us is immune to the lure of this message. Recently, a sharp-looking van in a television commercial caught my eye. Our family has a second-hand, 11-year-old station wagon painted an unattractive yellow. This advertised van was perfect for our family—just the right size and color. I even rationalized that this van would be better suited for use in ministry. I found myself spending

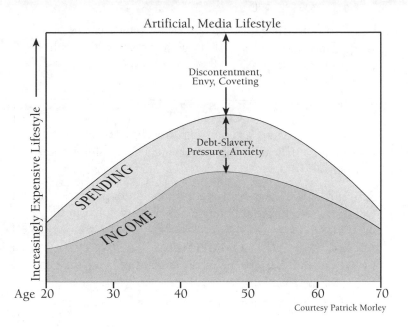

Courtesy Patrick Morley

half an hour each day studying beautiful, slick brochures, admiring new vans on the highway and daydreaming about driving one. I was hooked! The yellow station wagon seemed to get more unsightly every day, while the van went from an "I want it" to an "I need it" category.

I was about to buy the van when I decided to seek the counsel of Jack Norman, a local car dealer and friend. He gave me good advice. He asked me how many miles the station wagon had been driven. "Fifty-five thousand miles," I responded. He thought for a moment and then he said, "The station wagon is in good condition and should be great transportation for years!" I didn't want to hear that, but I reluctantly agreed with him. His advice had saved me thousands of dollars. Moreover, the moment the decision was made to keep the yellow station wagon, I lost the desire for the van. It no longer dominated my thinking. Interestingly enough, the yellow station wagon has become better-looking!

From time to time we all get hooked on something we think we must buy—a car, home, camera, boat, you name it. Once hooked, it is easy to rationalize a purchase. Please remember to seek the Lord's guidance and the counsel of a godly person when confronted with a spending decision.

CONTRAST

Society says: Acquire as many expensive possessions as possible because they are evidence you are a successful, important person.

Scripture says: The excessive accumulation of possessions will distract you from fulfilling God's purpose for your life.

COMMITMENT

I will prayerfully determine what standard of living the Lord wants for me.

PERSPECTIVE—
What's Really Important

A YOUNG ROGER MORGAN came out of the Appalachian Mountains with the sole purpose of making a fortune. Money became his god, and he became worth millions. Then the stock market crash of 1929 and the Great Depression reduced him to utter poverty. Penniless, he took to the road. One day a friend found him on the Golden Gate Bridge staring down into the waters of the San Francisco Bay, and he suggested they move on. "Leave me alone," Roger replied. "I'm trying to think. There is something more important than money, but I've forgotten what it is."

> The futility of riches is stated very plainly in two places: the Bible and the income tax form.

What Roger Morgan forgot, or perhaps never knew, was the scriptural perspective of money. That is what we will explore in this chapter.

MONEY WILL NOT BRING TRUE HAPPINESS

Solomon, the author of Ecclesiastes, had an annual income of more than $25 million. He lived in a palace that took 13 years to build.

He owned 40,000 stalls of horses. He sat on an ivory throne over-laid with gold. He drank from gold cups. The daily menu of his household included a 100 sheep and 30 oxen in addition to fallow-deer and fatted fowl.[7]

Obviously, Solomon was in a position to know whether money would bring happiness, and he did not hesitate to say that riches do not bring true happiness: "He who loves money shall never have enough. The foolishness of thinking that wealth brings happiness! The more you have, the more you spend, right up to the limits of your income" (Ecclesiastes 5:10-11, LB).

In contrast, most people believe you can buy happiness. The American Institute of Public Opinion found that 70 percent of Americans thought they would be happier if they could earn only $37 more a week. I find myself periodically siding with this major-ity, falling into the "if only" trap.

If only I had a new car, I would be satisfied. *If only* I lived in that nice house, I would be content. *If only* I had a particular job, I would be happy. The list is endless.

The Bible offers a sharp contrast to this attitude. As someone has said,

Money will buy:
A bed but not sleep;
Books but not brains;
Food but not an appetite;
A house but not a home;
Medicine but not health;
Amusement but not happiness;
A crucifix but not a Savior.

Is Money Evil?

Money is not evil. It is morally neutral. Money can be used for good, such as supporting missionaries or building hospitals. It also can be used for evil, such as financing illegal drugs and pornography.

Examine 1 Timothy 6:10 carefully: "The *love* of money is a root of all sorts of evil." The Bible does not condemn money itself, only the misuse of or a wrong attitude toward money. Moreover, particularly in the Old Testament, many of the godliest people were among the wealthiest people of the day. Job, Abraham and David were all wealthy, and yet they did not allow wealth to interfere with their relationship with the Lord.

Nevertheless, Scripture warns that riches can destroy a spiritually fruitful life. "And the one on whom seed was sown among the thorns, this is the man who hears the word, and the worry of the world, and the deceitfulness of riches choke the word, and it becomes unfruitful" (Matthew 13:22).

Also, it is easy for those who are rich to turn away from God. "For when I bring them into the land flowing with milk and honey, which I swore to their fathers, and they have eaten and are satisfied and become prosperous, then they will turn to other gods and serve them, and spurn Me and break My covenant" (Deuteronomy 31:20). Someone once observed, "For every 99 people who can be poor and remain close to Christ, only one can become wealthy and maintain close fellowship with Him." It must be human nature to cling to the Lord when it's obvious that only He can provide our needs. Once people become wealthy, they often take the Lord for granted because they no longer think they have as much need of Him.

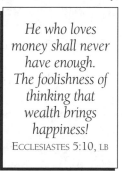

> *He who loves money shall never have enough. The foolishness of thinking that wealth brings happiness!*
> Ecclesiastes 5:10, LB

WILL GODLY PEOPLE ALWAYS PROSPER FINANCIALLY?

Some Christians embrace one of two extremes. Some say if you are really spiritual, you must be poor because wealth and a close relationship with Christ cannot coexist. The second and opposite extreme is the belief that if a Christian has faith, he or she will enjoy uninterrupted financial prosperity.

One end of the spectrum teaches that godliness can occur only in an environment of poverty. However, we already have noted that money is morally neutral and can be used for good or evil. In the Old Testament the Lord extended the reward of abundance to the children of Israel when they were obedient, while the threat of poverty was one of the consequences of disobedience. Deuteronomy 30:15, 16 reads, "I have set before you today life and prosperity, and death and adversity; in that I command you today to love the Lord your God, to walk in His ways and to keep His commandments . . . that the Lord your God may bless you."

Moreover, Psalm 35:27 reads, "The Lord . . . delights in the prosperity of His servant." We may also pray for prosperity when our relationship with the Lord is healthy. "Beloved, I pray that in all respects you may prosper and be in good health, just as your soul prospers" (3 John 2). Let me emphasize that again. The Bible does not say that a godly person *must* live in poverty. A godly person *may* have material resources.

There are those on the other hand who believe all Christians who truly have faith *always* will prosper. This extreme also is in error.

Study the life of Joseph. He is the classic example of a faithful person who experienced both prosperity and poverty. He was born into a prosperous family, then was thrown into a pit and sold into slavery by his jealous brothers. He became a household slave in a wealthy Egyptian's home. His master, Potiphar, promoted Joseph to head the household. Later Joseph made the righteous decision not to commit adultery with Potiphar's wife. Because of that decision, however, he was thrown into prison for years. In God's timing Joseph ultimately was elevated to the position of prime minister of Egypt.

Let's examine three reasons why the godly may not prosper.

1. Violating a Scriptural Principle

You may be giving generously but acting dishonestly. You may be honest but not properly fulfilling your work responsibilities. You may be a faithful employee but head-over-heels in debt. You may be completely out of debt but not giving.

One of the biggest benefits of this book is that we explore what the entire Bible teaches about money. Those who do not understand all the requirements may neglect critical areas of responsibility. If they suffer financially, they may be confused about the reason for their lack of prosperity.

2. Building of Godly Character

Romans 5:3-4 reads, "Tribulation brings about perseverance; and perseverance, proven character." An example of the Lord developing character in a people before prospering them is found in Deuteronomy 8:16-18:

> In the wilderness He fed you manna which your fathers did not know, that He might humble you and that He might test you, to do good for you in the end. Otherwise, you may say in your heart, "My power and the strength of my hand made me this wealth." But you shall remember the Lord your God, for it is He who is giving you power to make wealth.

The Lord knew the children of Israel had to be humbled before they could handle wealth. Our Father knows us better than we know ourselves. In His infinite wisdom He knows exactly how much He can entrust to us at any time without harming our relationship with Him.

3. The Mystery of God's Sovereignty

Hebrews 11:1-35 lists people who triumphed miraculously by exercising their faith in the living God. But in verse 36 the writer directs our attention abruptly to godly people who lived by faith and gained God's approval, yet experienced poverty. The Lord ultimately chooses how much to entrust to each person. And sometimes we simply can't understand or explain His decisions.

Let's summarize: The Scriptures teach neither the necessity of poverty nor uninterrupted prosperity. What the Bible teaches is the responsibility of being a faithful steward. Please review the following diagram and the contrasts between the three perspectives.

The Lord's Perspective of Prosperity

Before we leave the issue of prosperity, it is important to understand that the Lord's perspective of prosperity is contrary to that of our culture. The Lord evaluates true riches based on His spiritual value system. This contrast is stated most clearly in the book of Revelation. The godly poor are rich in God's sight. "I [the Lord] know your tribulation and your poverty (but you are rich)" (Revelation 2:9). Those who are wealthy yet do not enjoy a close relationship with Christ are actually poor. "Because you say, 'I am rich, and have become wealthy, and have need of nothing,' and you do not know that you are wretched and miserable and poor and blind and naked" (Revelation 3:17). True prosperity extends far beyond material possessions. True prosperity is gauged by how well we know Jesus Christ and by how closely we follow Him.

	Poverty	**Stewardship**	**Prosperity**
Possessions are	Evil	A responsibility	A right
I work to	Meet only basic needs	Serve Christ	Become rich
Godly people are	Poor	Faithful	Wealthy
Ungodly people are	Wealthy	Unfaithful	Poor
I give	Because I must	Because I love God	To get
My spending is	Without gratitude to God	Prayerful and responsible	Carefree and consumptive

INSTRUCTIONS TO THOSE WHO ARE RICH

Are you rich? Sometime I feel rich and sometimes I don't. It usually depends on whom I am around. Most of us define a rich person as a person who has more money than we do. But if we compare our living standards to all the people who have lived throughout history or even with the rest of the billions of people living on the earth today, the majority of us who live in this nation are rich.

The Lord knew the rich would face serious spiritual danger. So Scripture offers three instructions for "those who are rich in this present world" (1 Timothy 6:17).

1. Do not be conceited.

"Instruct those who are rich in this present world not to be conceited" (1 Timothy 6:17). Wealth tends to produce pride. For several years, I drove two vehicles. The first was an old pickup truck that cost $100. It looked as if it cost $100! When I drove that truck to the bank drive-in window to cash a check, I was humble. I knew the cashier was going to double-check my account to make certain that the driver of that truck had sufficient funds to cover the withdrawal. I waited patiently while she checked. When I received the money, I was so grateful. I drove away with a song in my heart and praises on my lips.

My other vehicle was a well-preserved, second-hand automobile that was expensive when it was new. When I drove that car to the bank, I appeared to be a different person. I deserved a certain amount of respect. I was not quite as patient when the cashier examined my account, and when I received the money, I was not as grateful. Wealth stimulates conceit.

James 1:9-10 addresses this issue: "But let the brother of humble circumstances glory in his high position; and let the rich man glory in his humiliation, because like flowering grass he will pass away." The poor should be encouraged as children of the King of kings, while the rich are to remain humble because life is short. If you are rich, you need the constant reminder to be humble before the Lord and other people.

2. Put no confidence in your assets.

"Instruct those who are rich in this present world not . . . to fix their hope on the uncertainty of riches, but on God, who richly supplies us with all things to enjoy" (1 Timothy 6:17). This has been a tremendous struggle for me. It is easy for us to trust in those tangible assets we have accumulated. I know that money can buy goods and services. It has so much power that it is easy to be fooled into thinking that money supplies our needs and offers security. Money can become our first love. We tend to trust in the seen rather than in the invisible living God. This is why we need to constantly remind ourselves to walk by faith rather than by sight.

3. Give generously.

"Instruct them to do good, to be rich in good works, to be generous and ready to share, storing up for themselves the treasure of a good foundation for the future, so that they may take hold of that which is life indeed" (1 Timothy 6:18-19).

As I suggested before, one of the most effective antidotes for the potential disease of loving money is "setting the finish line." Determine a maximum amount that you will accumulate. After you have reached your goal, give the rest to build God's kingdom.

CONTRAST

Society says: Wealth brings happiness and security, and I can use it for my own comfort any way I choose.

Scripture says: True joy is based on my relationship with Christ. In Him alone will I trust. If I am rich, I should be generous and ready to share.

COMMITMENT

I will consistently study the Bible to maintain God's perspective of money and possessions.

SUMMING IT ALL UP
LET'S REVIEW

AT THE BEGINNING of this book we asked why the Bible says so much about money—more than 2,350 verses. The Lord knew that how we handled money would help determine the intimacy of our fellowship with Him. The Lord also wanted to provide us a blueprint for handling money so that we could be faithful in this practical area of life.

> *There must be
> the conversion
> of the heart,
> the mind and also
> the purse.*
> MARTIN LUTHER

The fundamental truth for us to understand is that God has retained the responsibilities of ownership of possessions, control of events and provision of needs. As people, we are not designed to shoulder these responsibilities. However, the Lord delegated certain important tasks to us as stewards.

Review the diagram of the wheel and the eight areas of our responsibility.

Financial faithfulness is a journey—do not become discouraged.

Applying financial principles from Scripture is a journey that takes time. It's easy to become discouraged. When you finish this book, your finances may not be completely under control. Don't get frustrated. It takes the average person at least a year to apply most of these principles. Again, I want to encourage you to enroll in a Crown Ministries small group study. It is an excellent environment to receive encouragement and help in implementing these principles.

Faithfulness in small matters is important.
Because of a lack of resources many people become frustrated by their inability to solve their financial problems. Remember, simply be faithful with what you have—whether it is little or much.

Some give up too soon. They abandon the goal of becoming debt free. They stop trying to increase their saving or giving. For them the task seems impossible. And it may be impossible without the Lord's help. Your job is to make a genuine effort, no matter how small it may appear. Then leave the results to God. I love what the Lord said to the prophet Zechariah: "For who has despised the day of small things?" (Zechariah 4:10). Don't be discouraged. Be diligent. Be persistent. Be faithful in even the smallest matters.

A good friend once asked me what was the most valuable lesson I had learned from the Crown Ministries small group studies. I've had time to reflect on that question for some time now. I think the most valuable lesson has been the realization that I needed to consistently review Scripture. I noticed this in preparation for a class. If I had invested little time studying Scripture during the previous weeks, I would discover that I had been molded ever-so-subtly by the views of modern society. In Romans 12:2 Paul presented this problem and that solution: "And do not be conformed to this world, but be transformed by the renewing of your mind." The only way for any of us to renew our minds (to discover and preserve the correct perspective) is to expose ourselves to Scripture continually.

The Bible has the answers to the financial problems of the sophisticated twenty-first century. The eternal principles of Scripture are practical in any culture and in any century.

CONTENTMENT

At the beginning of this book I said that one of our objectives was that you would learn to be content. First Timothy 6:8 issues this challenging statement: "And if we have food and covering, with these we shall be content." Study this passage carefully. It declares that if you have food and covering (clothes and shelter), you should be content. Our culture has restated this verse to read something like this: "If you can afford the finest food to eat, wear the latest fashions, drive the newest luxury automobile and live in a beautiful home in the nicest section of town, then you can be happy." Nothing could be further from the truth.

There are three elements in learning to be content:

1. Know what God requires of a steward.
2. Fulfill those requirements faithfully.
3. Trust God to do His part.

Once we understand God's responsibilities and we have been faithful in fulfilling our responsibilities as stewards, we can be content. Our loving, heavenly Father will entrust us with the possessions He knows will be best for us at any particular time—whether much or little.

Biblical contentment is not to be equated with laziness, complacency, social insensitivity or apathy. Because we serve the living and dynamic God, Christians should always be improving. Contentment does not exclude properly motivated ambition. We already have discovered that God wants us to work hard. I believe we should have a burning desire to be faithful stewards of the talents and possessions He has entrusted to us. Biblical contentment is an inner peace that accepts what God has chosen for our present vocation, station in life and financial state. Hebrews 13:5 emphasizes this: "Let your character be free from the love of money, being content with what you have; for He Himself has said, 'I will never desert you, nor will I ever forsake you.'"

NOW IS THE TIME!

At the risk of being misunderstood by some, I would like to share a personal experience that helped shape my thinking and fueled my passion for helping people to become financially faithful. In 1977 I was alone in our kitchen. For the previous two years I had focused on studying what Scripture said about money. Suddenly, I was overcome by the Spirit of God and found myself prostrate on the kitchen floor, weeping. While I was on the floor, the Lord revealed to me that during my life our nation would experience a very difficult time economically. I don't know precisely when this will occur or what it will be like, but I believe God has graciously given us a window of time to conform to His Word in the area of money. I plead with you to seize this opportunity! Become diligent in your efforts to get out of debt, give generously, budget persistently and work as unto the Lord. In short, become a faithful steward.

You now know the biblical framework for managing money. But knowing is only half of the solution. You must act upon that knowledge. Jesus said,

> Every one who hears these words of Mine, and acts upon them, may be compared to a wise man, who built his house upon the rock. And the rain descended, and the floods came, and the winds blew, and burst against that house; and yet it did not fall, for it had been founded upon the rock. And every one who hears these words of Mine, and does not act upon them, will be like a foolish man, who built his house upon the sand. And the rain descended, and the floods came, and the winds blew, and burst against that house; and it fell, and great was its fall (Matthew 7:24-27).

The economic rain, floods and winds are gathering to burst against this nation's financial house. If you have built your house on the solid principles found in Scripture, your house will not fall. One of the best ways to demonstrate your love for your family and friends is to get your financial house in order and encourage others to do the same.

I appreciate the effort you have invested in reading this book. I pray this has given you a greater appreciation for the Scriptures, helped you put your financial house in order, and above all else, nurtured your love for Jesus Christ. May the Lord richly bless you in every way as you draw close to Him.

QUESTIONS AND ANSWERS

This section deals with some frequently asked and sometimes controversial questions. When Scripture does not specifically answer the question, my opinion is given to stir your thinking.

Question: What is God's perspective on paying taxes?

Answer: That's the same question that was asked of Jesus: "Is it lawful for us to pay taxes to Caesar, or not? . . . [Jesus] said to them, 'Show Me a denarius [Roman coin]. Whose head and inscription does it have?' And they said, 'Caesar's.' And He said to them, 'Then render to Caesar the things that are Caesar's'" (Luke 20:22-25).

This is a clear example of the contrast between the practices of our society and the teaching of Scripture. Avoid paying taxes at any cost, most people rationalize. After all, the government squanders much of the money it receives.

A very fine line often exists between tax avoidance and tax evasion, and many experience a strong temptation to misappropriate funds that are legally owed to the government. An estimated $100 billion a year in taxes is lost through tax evasion.

I am not condoning the waste and excesses found in government.

In fact, I believe a citizen should try to influence government to be more efficient and responsive. However, the Bible tells us of an additional responsibility: pay your taxes! "Let every person be in subjection to the governing authorities. For there is no authority except from God, and those which exist are established by God . . . because of this you also pay taxes, for rulers are servants of God, devoting themselves to this very thing. Render to all what is due them: tax to whom tax is due" (Romans 13:1, 6-7).

Question: How does the Bible define financial success?

Answer: According to Scripture, financial success is achieved by being a faithful steward. This is not the standard used by most people to judge success. Usually, the more wealth a person has accumulated, the more he or she is considered to have succeeded. However, according to Scripture it is impossible to tell if a person is truly "successful" by looking at his or her external circumstances, possessions or position. If we had seen Joseph or Paul in prison, Daniel in the lions' den or Job in his affliction, how many of us would have considered them successful?

Webster's definition of success is "the degree or measure of attaining a desired end." According to Scripture the desired end for us is to become faithful stewards. After we have fulfilled our responsibility by becoming faithful stewards, it is up to God to decide whether or not to entrust us with wealth.

Question: Is it permissible for a Christian to be ambitious?

Answer: Scripture does not condemn ambition. Paul was ambitious. "We have as our ambition . . . to be pleasing to Him. For we must all appear before the judgment seat of Christ, that each one may be recompensed for his deeds" (2 Corinthians 5:9-10).

What is strongly denounced is selfish ambition. The Lord "will render to every man according to his deeds . . . to those who are selfishly ambitious . . . wrath and indignation" (Romans 2:6-8). "But if you have . . . selfish ambition in your heart, do not be arrogant and so lie against the truth. This wisdom is not that which comes down from above, but is earthly, natural, demonic. For where . . . selfish ambition exist[s], there is disorder and every evil thing" (James 3:14-16).

The Bible is not the enemy of ambition, only of a wrong type of ambition. Our ambition should not be motivated out of an egotistical desire. "But you, are you seeking great things for yourself? Do not seek them" (Jeremiah 45:5). Our ambition should be to please Christ. We should have a burning desire to become increasingly faithful stewards in using the possessions and skills entrusted to us.

Question: Should wives work in a job outside the home?

Answer: The trend for wives to hold jobs outside a home is escalating rapidly. In 1947 working husbands outnumbered working wives five to one; now the ratio is less than two to one.

For many reasons, women are involved in jobs of all kinds. Married women work to provide additional income for their families, to express their creativity or to enjoy the work environment. Widows and divorcees often must work to provide for their needs. A Stanford University study shows that wives who work outside the home carry a particularly heavy load of responsibility. With their job and their household activities, these wives work 70 to 80 hours a week.

In my opinion, during children's early formative years it is preferable for a mother to be home whenever the children are home. Titus 2:4-5 reads, "Encourage the young women to love their husbands, to love their children, to be sensible, pure, workers at home." It is ideal for a mother of young children to limit working outside the home to those times when the children are not at home unless family finances depend upon her income. As children mature, the wife will have increased freedom to pursue work outside the home. Proverbs 31:10-27 reads,

> An excellent wife . . . does him [her husband] good and not evil all the days of her life. She looks for wool and flax, and works with her hands . . . She brings her food from afar. She rises also while it is still night, and gives food to her household . . . She considers a field and buys it; from her earnings she plants a vineyard . . . She stretches out her hands to the

distaff, and her hands grasp the spindle. She extends her hand to the poor . . . She makes coverings for herself; her clothing is fine linen and purple. Her husband is known in the gates, when he sits among the elders of the land. She makes linen garments and sells them, and supplies belts to the tradesmen . . . She looks well to the ways of her household, and does not eat the bread of idleness.

Proverbs 31 paints a beautiful picture of the working wife living a balanced life with the thrust of her activity toward the home. My opinion is that a wife's work is not so much in the home as it is for the home. The Bible does not say that a wife should be confined to four walls, but rather it describes a woman involved in activities that relate to the home.

Some women are gifted as homemakers. However, other women have the aptitude and desire to work outside the home. Whether or not a wife works outside a home is a decision that the husband and wife should make prayerfully and with full agreement.

If a wife works to produce more income for a family, it is important to analyze exactly how much income, after taxes and expenses, her work contributes to the family. Couples often are surprised to learn that this income is not as much as they had expected.

Question: What does the Bible tell us about partnerships?

Answer: Second Corinthians 6:14-17 reads,

Do not be bound together [unequally yoked] with unbelievers; for what partnership have righteousness and lawlessness, or what fellowship has light with darkness? Or what harmony has Christ with Belial, or what has a believer in common with an unbeliever? Or what agreement has the temple of God with idols? For we are the temple of the living God; just as God said, "I will dwell in them and walk among them; and I will be their God, and they shall be My people. Therefore, come out from their midst and be separate," says the Lord.

Scripture clearly discourages business partnerships with those who do not know Christ. Many have violated this principle and have suffered financially.

In my opinion we also should be very careful before entering into a partnership with another Christian. I would consider only a few people as potential partners. I have known these individuals for years and have observed their commitment to the Lord. I know their strengths and weaknesses and have seen them consistently handle money faithfully. *Do not rush into a partnership!* Prayerfully evaluate what it may entail.

Before forming a partnership, reduce your understandings and agreements into written form with your future partner. In this written document provide a method to dissolve the partnership if necessary. If you are not able to agree in writing, do not become partners.

Question: Why do the wicked prosper?

Answer: This is a disturbing question God's people have asked for centuries. The prophet Jeremiah inquired of the Lord. "You are always righteous, O Lord, when I bring a case before you. Yet I would speak with you about your justice: Why does the way of the wicked prosper? Why do all the faithless live at ease?" (Jeremiah 12:1, NIV).

The Psalmist also asked why the wicked prospered, and he admitted being envious of them. Godliness did not seem to "pay off." Then the Lord revealed the wicked person's end—sudden eternal punishment.

> Surely God is good to . . . those who are pure in heart. But as for me, my feet had almost slipped . . . for I envied the arrogant when I saw the prosperity of the wicked. They have no struggles . . . Therefore pride is their necklace . . . When I tried to understand all this, it was oppressive to me till I entered the sanctuary of God; then I understood their final destiny. Surely you place them on slippery ground; you cast them down to ruin. How suddenly are they destroyed, completely swept away by terrors! (Psalm 73:1-19, NIV).

The Bible tells us that some of the wicked will prosper, but it does not say why they prosper. However, what the Lord does tell us is not to worry. Do not envy the wicked person who prospers, because life on earth is so short that he will fade away quickly. "Do not fret because of evil men or be envious of those who do wrong; for like the grass they will soon wither, like green plants they will soon die away" (Psalm 37:1-2, NIV). We are encouraged to maintain the Lord's eternal perspective with His eternal value system.

Question: What does the Bible say about lawsuits?

Answer: More than 22,000 civil lawsuits are filed each day in our nation! Unfortunately, many of these suits pit Christian against Christian at an annual cost of millions of dollars.

Suing seems to be a national pastime: A woman from Maryland sued a man who she said kicked her at a dance. She sought $200,000 as compensation for the injury and time lost on the dance floor. A former professional football player was awarded $300,000 for the "psychological injury" he suffered from being called a "chicken" by the team doctor.

There are a number of reasons for this flood of lawsuits, including an avalanche of new laws and regulations. More disturbing, people are becoming less and less forgiving.

The current court system uses an adversarial judicial process, which frequently creates animosities and fractures relationships between the parties involved. Instead of trying to heal the wounds, the system provides a technical and legal solution to the case but leaves the problems of unforgiveness and anger untouched. The overriding objective in litigation is to win.

Yet the Bible stresses that the goal should be reconciliation. "If therefore you are presenting your offering at the altar, and there remember that your brother has something against you, leave your offering there before the altar, and go your way; first be reconciled to your brother" (Matthew 5:23-24).

Scripture states clearly that when Christians are at odds with one another, they should not settle their disputes through the secular courts.

Does any one of you, when he has a case against his neighbor, dare to go to law before the unrighteous, and not before the saints? Or do you not know that the saints will judge the world? And if the world is judged by you, are you not competent to constitute the smallest law courts? Do you not know that we shall judge angels? How much more, matters of this life? If then you have law courts dealing with matters of this life, do you appoint them as judges who are of no account in the church? I say this to your shame. Is it so, that there is not among you one wise man who will be able to decide between his brethren, but brother goes to law with brother, and that before unbelievers? Actually, then, it is already a defeat for you, that you have lawsuits with one another. Why not rather be wronged? Why not rather be defrauded? (1 Corinthians 6:1-7).

Instead of initiating a lawsuit, a three-step procedure for Christians to resolve their differences is set forth in Matthew 18:15-17: "And if your brother sins, go and reprove him in private; if he listens to you, you have won your brother. But if he does not listen to you, take one or two more with you, so that by the mouth of two or three witnesses every fact may be confirmed. And if he refuses to listen to them, tell it to the church; and if he refuses to listen even to the church, let him be to you as a Gentile and a tax gatherer."

1. Go in private. The party who believes he has been wronged needs to confront the other person in private with his claims. If the dispute remains unresolved, then . . .

2. Go with one or two others. The person who feels wronged should return with witnesses who can confirm facts or help resolve the dispute. If this is still unsuccessful, then . . .

3. Go before the church. The third step is mediation or arbitration before an impartial group in the church or perhaps a local Christian mediation service, if this is available in your area.

The greatest benefit of following this procedure is not simply reaching a fair settlement of the dispute, but practicing forgiveness, fostering peace and demonstrating love.

Question: What does the Lord say about favoritism (partiality)?

Answer: The Bible is clear. Study carefully James 2:1-9,

> My brethren, do not hold your faith in our glorious Lord
> Jesus Christ with an attitude of personal favoritism. For if a
> man comes into your assembly with a gold ring and dressed
> in fine clothes, and there also comes in a poor man in dirty
> clothes, and you pay special attention to the one who is wear-
> ing the fine clothes, and say, "You sit here in a good place,"
> and you say to the poor man, "You stand over there, or sit
> down by my footstool," have you not made distinctions
> among yourselves, and become judges with evil motives?
> Listen, my beloved brethren: did not God choose the
> poor of this world to be rich in faith and heirs of the king-
> dom which He promised to those who love Him? But you
> have dishonored the poor man. Is it not the rich who
> oppress you and personally drag you into court? Do they not
> blaspheme the fair name by which you have been called? If,
> however, you are fulfilling the royal law, according to the
> Scripture, "You shall love your neighbor as yourself," you are
> doing well. But if you show partiality, you are committing
> sin and are convicted by the law as transgressors.

I have struggled with the sin of partiality. I would not be so
obvious as to tell one to stand and another to sit in a favored place,
but in my heart I have often been guilty of favoritism, and this has
unintentionally influenced my actions. Once, when I hung up the
phone, my wife said, "I know you were not talking to Ken; it must
have been Ryan. You like Ken better, and it shows in your voice."

Partiality does not have to be based on a person's wealth. It can
also be based on a person's education, social position in the community or spiritual status in the church. James 2:9 could not be
more direct: "But if you show partiality, *you are committing sin* and
are convicted by the law as transgressors." How do we break the
habit of partiality?

Romans 12:10 tells us, "Be devoted to one another in brotherly love; give preference to one another in honor." And Philippians 2:3 reads, "With humility of mind let each of you regard one another as more important than himself." We need to ask the Lord to ingrain in our thinking the habit of elevating each person consistently and consciously, regardless of his or her station in life, as more important than ourselves. One practical way to overcome partiality is to concentrate on the strengths and abilities of each person. Every person can do some things better than I can. This realization helps me appreciate all people.

Question: What does the Bible say about coveting?

Answer: Coveting means to desire or crave another person's property. Coveting is expressly prohibited throughout Scripture. The last of the Ten Commandments reads, "You shall not covet your neighbor's house; you shall not covet your neighbor's wife or his male servant or his female servant or his ox or his donkey or anything that belongs to your neighbor" (Exodus 20:17). That commandment ends with an infinitely broad prohibition: *"or anything that belongs to your neighbor."* In other words, we are commanded not to covet anything that belongs to anyone!

Greed is similar to coveting. "But do not let immorality or any impurity or greed even be named among you. . . . For this you know with certainty, that no immoral or impure person or covetous man, who is an idolater, has an inheritance in the kingdom of Christ and God" (Ephesians 5:3-5).

A greedy or covetous person is an idolater. Coveting and greed have been called the universal, silent sins. Rarely are they addressed or confronted, but I believe they are among the most widespread sins of this generation. When I began studying what the Bible teaches about money, I was overwhelmed by the extent of my own coveting. Ask the Lord to show you if you are guilty of coveting that which is another's. If you are, repent and submit to the Holy Spirit. Ask Him to change your heart.

Question: Should we give to secular charities?

Answer: Numerous secular charities (such as schools, fraternal orders or organizations formed to conquer various diseases) compete vigorously for our gift dollars. Scripture does not address whether or not we should give to these charities. However, Bev and I have decided not to normally support these organizations with our gifts. Our reason is that while many people support secular charities, only those who know the Lord support the ministries of Christ. We have occasionally given to secular charities when we sensed the Lord's prompting to give or when the solicitor was a friend we wanted to encourage or influence for Christ.

Question: The Scriptures repeatedly prohibit idolatry. How is that applicable in our modern age?

Answer: Few people today bow before stone pillars or golden statues. That form of idolatry is a thing of the past. However, we are always in danger of substituting other things in the place of God and of devoting to them the affection which is due Him alone. Practical idolatry is everywhere. As someone said, "Most idols today have four wheels, tinted glass, chrome and baked-on enamel." God should have first place in our hearts. His perspective should influence every descision we make. Everything should be subordinated to our love of Him. If we love anything—family, job or possessions more than the Lord, it is an idol.

NOTES

1. Charles L. Allen, *God's Psychiatry* (Old Tappan, NJ: Revell, 1953).
2. David McConaughy, *Money, the Acid Test* (Philadelphia: Westminster Press, 1918), pp. 24, 25.
3. Richard Halverson, *Perspective* (Los Angeles: Cowman Publications, 1957), p. 59.
4. George Fooshee, *You Can Be Financially Free* (Old Tappan, NJ: Revell, 1976), p. 26.
5. Herb Goldberg and Robert Lewis, *Money Madness* (New York: Morro, 1978), pp. 13, 14.
6. Randy Alcorn, *Money, Possessions and Eternity* (Wheaton, IL, Tyndale House Publishers), p. 128, 129.
7. Leslie B. Flynn, *Your God and Your Gold* (Grand Rapids: Zondervan), p. 112.